INSIDE

C000199753

Personal Excellence through Self Discovery - 9 Steps to Radically Changing Your Life

Some people fight to survive . . .

Other's live lives . . .

Some people dare to dream . . .

And others step out and CREATE

the life of their dreams . . .

Which one are YOU?

Why not join the club?

Paperback ISBN 978-1-907685-67-5

ePub ISBN 978-1-907685-68-2

Mobipocket/Kindle ISBN 978-1-907685-69-9

Published in the UK by MX Publishing

335 Princess Park Manor, Royal Drive, London, N11 3GX

www.mxpublishing.co.uk

Cover design by www.staunch.com

This book is dedicated to the people who dare to make their life the biggest game in the world to them, and in doing so, dare to make a difference in the lives of others.

To those who have the courage to step out and make change so that they can live the life that they were born to live rather than let their live's be lived by their situations. To those who become conscious creators of every single thing that they do and to share their message with everyone that they come into contact with.

We pray that this book gives you the secrets to creating change and thereby creating a world that you can be proud of.

Thank you

ACKNOWLEDGEMENTS

This book would not have come about had it not been for some pretty influential people who have come into our lives over the years, and to so many other people who have had an impact on us. If your name is not mentioned here, it is not intentional; you are always in our thoughts on a daily basis.

(G) To My own Personal God – you gave me more than a second chance to live my life as you gave it to me. Thank you for believing in me and loving me before I even thought I had it in me.

(G) To Jeroen – my business partner, one of the closest friends I have ever had and my "brother from another mother." Without you, this book would be packed away in a box collecting dust. Thank you for sharing similar dreams and this journey with me. Long may it prosper and grow.

 (G) To Mandi – My Bean. I love you and that is all. Together, we went through so much and I would not be the man that I am today had I not had someone like you in my life. You gave me 2 very precious gifts, but more than that, you went through most of this with me.

(G) To Darryn and Savannah – 2 of the most amazing blessings God could ever have given to me. You inspire me daily to live my life to its full potential and you make everything worthwhile for me

(G) To Mom – without you, I would not be here today and that is that really. The most amazing mom in the whole world, you worked so hard to provide for us and you showed me what can be done when everything is gone. I love you.

(G) To Kerpy Gum – where do I start? My little sister who was always the strong one. The one who brought me chocolates and food. The one who sat and changed my bandages when I was too afraid to go to anyone else. The one who brought me to England for the very first time, knowing that it would change my life. Thank you for everything.

(G) To Andy "Dude" Pape – Duuuuuuuuuuuuddddddeee !!!!!!!! You truly showed me how to lighten up and have fun, no matter what the situation, no matter where you were or who you were with.

(G) To Merie and Luca – thank you for allowing me to be a part of your family.

(G) To Dave "Doc" Humphreys – thank you for opening up your home to me and allowing it to be mine too. For sharing your family with me, but also for sharing your philosophy on life with me.

(G) To My "12-Step Gang" – Claire (Poffadder), Tim, Sarah, Jan and all the other members – the meetings, the discussions, the arguments, the laughter and the tears, the hospital visits, the late night calls. It was here that I learnt the most about myself.

(G) To Jorge Sousa – the first man I ever fell in love with, but more than that, the man who got me to fall in love with myself. You will always have a truly special place in my heart my friend.

(G) To Keziah Smit – this book is a tribute to the courage you showed me and to how you lived your life. You will be in my memories forever and long may you fly with the angels you so fondly spoke about.

(G) To Dan Ardebili – your coaching calls pushed so many buttons and your humble knowledge opened up a whole new way of life for me

(G) To Dan Bradbury and Kevin Hall – the tools you teach to people truly take their businesses to another level. Sometimes, I guess, it just takes a bit longer for some of us to realise that they apply to us too.

(G) To Rob Gardini – you taught me everything I know about construction, and not just of buildings. Through everything, you also supported me and encouraged me like your own son and you taught me how a strong foundation was more important than anything else you could ever build.

(J) To my parents, Jeannette and Louis – without you, I would not be who I am and where I am today. Thank you.

(J) To my brother, Dennis – you have been a huge role model to me, even without you even noticing it.

(J) To my cousin, Pascal – you showed me how to connect with my soul and will be with me forever.

(J) To my grandparents – thank you for showing me so much love and warmth.

(J) To my partner Merie – you always believe in me and have given me the greatest gift of all – our son. Thank you for being the best mother in the world.

(J) To Gareth – for just being himself and helping me to be me.

(G & J) To Amy Brann – you have supported and encouraged both of us every step of the way and you have shared so much of your knowledge with us.

(G & J) To Johnnie Cass, Duane Alley, Peter Shaw and Christopher Howard – some of the greatest teachers and mentors to have come our way. You all pushed us to limits I never thought achievable, and then past that too.

(G & J) To our family at ThinkBig Education – Kate, Dan, Caroline, Jeanine, Monika, Marcos, George, Emma, Shani, Tamar, all the friends we have met during the trainings, the Crew and AV Guys and everyone in Australia – thank you for what you do in making the world an amazing place

And to the people that neither of us know personally, but who have had a great influence in our lives and are a daily inspiration in all that we do: -

- Anthony Robbins
- Dr John DeMartini
- Deepak Chopra
- Robin Sharma
- Jim Rohn
- Paulo Coehlo
- Robert Kiyosaki
- Martin Luther King Jnr
- Sir Richard Branson

A Brief Introduction

First of all, thank you for taking the time out to open this book and to share this experience. It has been an absolute joy, and at times a total challenge, to get these words out onto paper, but nonetheless, it has been a mind blowing experience. I guess you could say it has been a trip down memory lane in some respects and at the same time, it has also brought back to mind the fundamental steps that were taken to change lives.

What started off as a solo journey some time back has changed over the last few months of writing. But more importantly, it has been instrumental in the final piece of this book coming to light and sharing itself with the world. It has always been my lifelong dream to share how I changed my life and created something out of nothing and this is the start of it all.

This book is a guide to the steps that we took; the learning's that we had along the way and the culmination of over 10 years of intense studying, self exploration, learning, applying, practising and doing. Throughout the journey, and in each "chapter" we will share with you stories from our lives and at the same time, get to know you as well.

I used to think "Why is it that some people achieve all that they set out to do and yet some people lag behind, wondering what went wrong, why they did not get what they may have planned out for their lives or what went wrong along the way?"

In some cases, people may not even realise that they have the choice to make something out of their lives and tend to walk the path that has been laid out before them, totally unaware of the possibilities out there and the many directions they have available for them to choose from.

For part of my life, I travelled that safe road, blissfully unaware what was going on around me and "taking things in my stride" until one day, I woke up from that life and made a choice – what do I do next? And so I began my journey into the "unknown world" and began really living a life that I wanted to create for myself. I learnt lessons, accepted that I would make mistakes but more importantly, I began to live what I could actually call a life of my own, and it was for this reason that I decided to share with you what has helped me along the way, and also to invite you on a journey.

I hope that this book brings together what has helped me along the way in the hope that it will give you guidance and assistance into creating your own journey. It will give you a comprehensive insight into your own life, as well as a practical way into designing your own compelling future. For those of you that are new to personal excellence, it will provide you with things that you may never have thought of looking at before, and for those that are already familiar with self discovery, it will give you some helpful and practical tips in a new light.

These are tools and techniques that I have been using every day to set out and achieve my own dreams and promises, and I know that they will give you everything you now need to set out on your own adventure into the beyond.

CONTENTS

WHAT'S WITH THE TITLE?

Before we go any further, maybe it would be a good idea to tell you about the title of this book. I haven't had a dull life, and at the same time, I have not had the most terrible life, however, I have had been through a lot and would not want anyone to go through some of the things that I have been through. I have made some good choices and I have also made some seriously crazy ones that when I look back, I just shake my head.

During 2008, one of THE MOST TRANSFORMATIONAL YEARS OF MY LIFE, as I was on the brink of making some life changing decisions yet again, going though the processes that I am about to share with you, I met an amazing man who changed my life in an instant and became possibly one of the closest friends, brothers, colleagues and now business partners I have ever had.

I guess that you could also say that this book is a tribute to the final missing piece of the puzzle in my life and where I am today as well. His knowledge and wisdom, combined with everything that I have learnt and since shared with him, has had a profound impact in the way I choose to live today. For both of us, it has been that one little thing that neither of us could quite put our fingers on in our search for personal excellence in our own lives.

Jeroen and I met initially at a training we were both attending, and for me, it was here that I decided to face one of my greatest fears – I guess you could say I wanted to "stand up to the school bully" for want of a better word. And I made it my intention to sit down and have a discussion with him. Over the next few months, we met every now and then at further courses and also worked together at events we used to volunteer at, and still do to this day. We gradually started talking about more and more stuff, and one evening, had a frank and honest discussion about what it was that we wanted to do with our lives.

It is not very often that you meet someone who is so physically different to you, yet at the same time, almost identical. And upon sharing more, it is not very often that you meet people so similarly aligned with the same visions for what they want to achieve in their lives based upon the instrumental foundation upon which everything in life is built – being truly authentic and living from the heart. Yet it happened and so things developed and grew and our baby – Ego Invenio – was born and our lives were turned inside out.

One more important, and possibly one of the most vital points I could add, is that there was one very striking similarity we both held in our lives. For most of our working lives, in different parts of the world, both of us have been involved in construction. In fact, until recent decisions to radically change careers, it has been the only profession either of us has worked in since a very young age. One of us worked on the "nuts and bolts" of the buildings, in other words, seeing exactly what is required to ensure the best possible building can be built, from the quantity of bricks, doors and floor tiles to the finances required to fund such a project and communicating with all parties involved from architects to engineers, suppliers to sub contractors. And the other worked on making the building water proof and tight, looking amazing from the outside so that the building itself could stand tall and proud. And if any of you know a little bit about construction, both of these are fundamentally vital to any building.

In life, we always have choices. We grow up being taught by our family, our society, people who have gone before us because that is what they have learnt along their journeys. For some people, this is OK, and then for others – you know, those people that we read about, who do amazing things – they appear to have "something different" from everyone else that we strive to achieve. We model and study them, we watch what they do and yes, sometimes it works, but at the same time, as we look around us, we see people carrying on the way we are shown.

We do not know about you, but we have always known that there is so much more out there and have spent many years searching and learning, fighting the traditional ways of society and education, fiercely dedicated to discovering everything we could. We knew that what we had in our lives was (and is) just the tip of the iceberg and that we have the basic fundamental freedom of choice to do with our lives whatever it is that we choose.

Imagine for a few minutes now if you would, what it would be like if you could: -

- **Unleash and learn to express your true potential through your lifestyle, work and relationships?**
- *Learn skills to create awareness and connection between your mind, body and emotions for improved health, happiness and well being?*
- **Become a conscious creator of your own life instead of simply reacting to what comes along?**
- *Discover your natural leadership qualities and express them in all that you do?*
- **Radically transform your physical life so that you experience massive strides in your personal energy levels?**
- *Restore focus, clarity and peace of mind in your business and personal life?*
- **Live your life with passion through self acceptance and awareness at a deep level?**
- *Achieve balance in all areas of your life so that every day is an adventure of discovery and excitement?*

The best investment you can make (time, money and resources) in your own life is in yourself. If you do not have a solid foundation upon which to build anything we choose, no matter how hard you work, you are not going to achieve the level of results and satisfaction that you were naturally born to attain.

And that foundation is you as a whole – physically, mentally, emotionally and spiritually.

PHYSICALLY – the ability to transform your body and your life

MENTAL & EMOTIONAL – energy follows thought and you get what you think about, whether you like it or not

SPIRITUALLY – gain access to your God given wisdom and power, trust your inner guidance and force and listen to your heart which is your truest wisdom

And this is what EGO INVENIO is all about!

This book started out as one of us (Gareth) sharing his journey through life yet contains the basic principles upon which everything we, as Ego Invenio, do and stand for. Things change and grow but the message remains the same.

Anyone can turn their life inside out, no matter how far down the road they have chosen to travel. All that matters is that they take a stand and begin to excel at everything they are. But more importantly, it is a tribute to what can be done when you let go and trust – not only yourself, but other people as well. And we hope and pray that by following our simple process, you begin your own journey to personal excellence through self discovery too.

A WORD FROM EACH OF US

Before we carry on any further, we would both like to share with you what everything in Ego Invenio means to us as individuals and we are sure that it will give you more of an insight into the message that we want to share with the world.

JEROEN

It feels like my whole life has been moving towards this point.

- **The point of decision**
- *The point of playing a bigger game*
- **The point of facing the fear and doing it anyway**
- *The point of focus and action*

I really ran out of excuses for not doing what I know I should have been doing. I am being pushed from different directions, but all together in one and the same direction. The direction of helping people discover who they really are and meant to be, to be able to live a happy, healthy and fulfilling life - on purpose.

For the biggest part of my life, people have seen me as a confident and healthy person, whilst in reality I wasn't. The fact that people see you as confident does not really help, as they expect you to be able to step up and speak out. Because of this dilemma, the conversations in my head became louder and were not very positive or uplifting. Instead of praising or congratulating myself for achievements or gains, I became very good at beating myself up. And as a result of this, I was not saying the things that I felt I should say and kept playing small, feeling like I was not worth much at all.

I started focusing more and more on my appearance and looks. That way I camouflaged my insecurity. So I felt stupid, but at least I looked good. I became some sort of an Ice-Man or robot; not showing anything of what was going on inside of me. Although I believe that we need to make the most out of life, I was definitely not doing it myself. That hurts! Although it does help to keep you small!

From a young age I've been inspired by the riddles of life. I went through many trainings, read books, and went to seminars to develop, grow and evolve as a human and spiritual being. I got to know many laws and sciences that help you to develop and take more control over your life. At one of the trainings I met Gareth who became a dear friend and brother and is now my business partner. Gareth is someone that has been working on those areas that I did not want to face for a long time. He has been working on the inside such as self-acceptance, but while he was working so hard on the inside, he did not focus on his physical well being and appearance. The Outside!

When we found out and realised how similar and aligned we were, though yet focusing on completely different areas, we realised the power of the combination of the two. He helped me to accept myself, loosen-up, or how he nicely puts it:"Stand up straight, on the inside!" I helped him on the outside, and made him realise how important your physical health is, and how to be proud and stand up straight on the outside.

We are both of the opinion (because of personal experience) that one is not working without the other. To move successfully forward in life, we need both! We require a strong foundation to be able to build a beautiful and strong construction that shines and lasts. With the knowledge and experience we have and our combined passion of inspiring and helping people to live a healthy and fulfilling life, we came up with the concept of Ego Invenio.

We don't believe in "Personal Development", because we believe that we are perfect as we are. Everything we need to be successful is already within us. It is about remembering and discovering who we really are.

EGO = I

INVENIO = Discovery

We are here to guide you on a journey of Personal Excellence through Self Discovery. Thanks for being you and thanks for being here.

GARETH

I have been asking myself my favourite question – "WHY?"

Why is this challenging me and why is it difficult to get this out?

Now I know that for some people, this is probably the "wrong" question to ask, but then I look at the results I have in my own life and I see, now, how I have the results that I have on a deep and structural level. I have never been one to do things normally – I suppose you could say I do everything the "hard" way just to make sure that it works. And I know that it works because I have the long lasting results in my life. I get them at a deep level and am finding it easier and easier to share with people what has transformed my life, so much so, that I sometimes do not recognise it and that's pretty cool.

Today, I was taking my daily look at people who inspire me to share my message, and one of them is a young internet marketer. He asked the question "What did you want to be when you grew up?" and that simple question got me to accept what this decision, and what Ego Invenio truly means to me.

As long as I can remember, I have always worked on my internal world. Because I saw myself as a weak person, not able to stand up straight in life,

I knew that faith and courage were the corner stone to everything that I wanted to do. Yet at the same time, thanks to what I chose to believe about my situations, I never believed that I could stand up straight. That got me working even harder on what I had inside of me.

It was difficult because when you want to be seen as a strong person, you actually doubt what you have to say and share as I felt that it was nothing special. And because I could not accept myself deep down inside, my physical health suffered which then had a negative impact on my inner health so it was the constant viscous cycle of always beating myself – physically, mentally and emotionally – just to push myself even further. I knew deep down inside that I had a gift to share yet as I could not physically see myself as a strong person, I began making decisions based on blind faith and passion for what I wanted out of life.

A few years ago, I made another life changing decision to take the next giant leap towards living my dream and sharing my message. I met Jeroen who was someone that was a physical representation of "people" who used to make fun of me in the past for wanting to do something.

As I got to know him more and more, I began to see something that terrified me to own and admit at first. Here was a man who, to me, was what I used to believe I wanted to be seen as – healthy, physically and mentally fit and strong and someone who was not afraid to say what he had to say. Yet at the same time, I knew this guy and am now very proud and grateful to say that he is my closest friend, brother and business partner. He showed me that when I spoke from the heart, huge changes take place because I saw them happen in his life.

I never found anyone who believed in such similar life principles and philosophies – of going on a journey to find out exactly who we are and to live it. I saw him change and grow as a result of conversations we had, and at the same time, I began to physically change my life. I started to be healthier, I began standing up straight and holding my head proud, but more importantly than anything else, I finally accepted that what I thought was "nothing special" in the past was actually quite life changing.

We learnt that one could not go without the other.

We saw that no matter how hard you work on the inside, if you do not apply that same work to the outside, there is nothing. Without a rock solid foundation, it does not matter what mindset or skill you have in life, your results would only be magnified by this foundation.

Ego Invenio is a journey to unlock something you know is missing to radically change the way you live your life, and to me, this is the easiest, yet possibly biggest decision, I have ever made in my life and it is thank to trusting, opening up and standing up tall and proud, inside and out.

INTRODUCTION

All I could do was lie there and fight. It felt like I had been tied to the bed, my arms and legs stuck in some sort of gross restraint contraption – you know, like when you have one of those dreams where you just can't move but you have to get away from whatever it is that is chasing you? You can't actually see what is coming, yet you know that if you do not move, then it is going to get you. That is how I felt – this bad dream that I just could not wake up from and the more I tried to move, the tighter the restraints came. At the same time, I had the overwhelming urge to go and have a pee – my bladder felt like it was going to burst at any minute and I didn't think that I could hold it in for much longer. And to make matters even worse, there was this irritatingly annoying beeping going off in my ear – beep, beep, beep. Fucking irritating if you ask me.

My head was pounding as well. One of those headaches that you get after a huge bender of whatever was going for the day.

"Gareth, stop moving about so much" someone kept telling me. Well if you could actually move when you tried then maybe you would stop bloody struggling I tried to say but all I could do was some sort of garbled moan, and somewhat painful at that as well.

What the fuck is going on I thought to myself because let me tell you, this ain't no dream. For some reason, I actually am tied to this bed and for the same reason, I cannot move to go and have that pee and that is when it dawned on me what the hell was going on.

Again!

Fucking again!

Except this time it was bad, very bad.

I wouldn't say that it was anger that came over me; I would probably say that it was rage – driving ugly rage that filled me from wherever it came. Why, why did you have to wake up I said to myself, just why. Enough is enough and now this, no matter how hard I try, it won't go away – this thing inside me that wants to eat me, this thing inside me that drives me crazy every single day of my life, this thing that won't go away no matter how much I drink or shovel up my nose or down my throat or even smoke, and here I am. Here I am again. Only this time physically tied to a bed, naked, covered in a sheet with wires and tubes coming from all over the place – a machine angrily beeping at me with every beat of my heart telling me that I am still here, that I am still taking up space on the planet, that I am still hurting my family – AGAIN !

You know what I screamed, if you don't let me off this bed I am going to piss everywhere – only I don't think that that is what it sounded like to the nurse sitting there. She looked at me and pleaded again "Please Gareth, stop moving about, it will only hurt you more" and that was just the cherry on the top. I had to pee because I couldn't hold it in anymore so I just did – there, in my bed, all over the place. Who cares I thought, because I don't anymore. And then it went dark again – that peaceful place where things are OK, where the darkness takes you over again. But this time, it wasn't peaceful and it wasn't a safe place – people had come in and seen what was going on inside of me and now that I had failed at this dismal attempt to end it all I had to do something. Only I just was not sure what I could do.

The night before came flooding back to me, in fact the few weeks or months before had come flooding back to me and now I had to face it all.

It seemed like only a few minutes later that I opened my eyes again, only to look up and see a familiar face – and not just one either. Their faces were puffy and eyes were bloodshot from crying and I could see the pain and fear in their eyes. And that made the tears come to my eyes too – I wanted to hug them but was too scared, and besides, I was still tied to the godamn bloody bed, I could not move my arms and my face hurt to move from the tubes shoved into me. If you have never had a tube shoved down your nose and throat to keep you breathing and pump your stomach clear of shit, I would not recommend it. To think that something that size actually fits up your nose makes my eyes water just at the thought of it. And it goes down your throat so that every time you try and move your head, you feel it move around so you just lie there, keeping as still as you can. But then you cry, and when you cry you also want to swallow that lump that builds up in your throat and yeah, that is pretty painful too I might add. So you just do what you can – it makes sense now why that poor nurse was pleading with me to keep still.

"I'm sorry" I tried to say but who the heck knows what came out. It was only later on when I found out that I had been like that for a number of days, them not knowing if I would make it, that I realised how stupid those words must have sounded. After all, less than six months ago I had promised that I would never try anything like that again and I would never put them through it again and yet lo and behold, here I was except this time much worse for wear than before – this time I had almost not been so lucky to wake up had it not been for a heavily pregnant friend finding me lying in my underwear, going blue and hardly breathing – had she arrived at my home half an hour later, I would not have been tied to that bed.

They tell you things later on about what happened and I had to sit through it and listen. I had taken so many tablets that they had begun to eat the lining of my stomach and there was nothing to pump. Had they arrived, like I said earlier, half an hour later to take me to the hospital, I would not have made it. I had been in a drug induced coma for almost 7 days, connected to monitors and machines, my family not knowing whether I would make it – my wife, my 7 year old son and my 3 year old daughter not knowing what they had done to make me do something so stupid, my mom and my sister desperately worried about what the hell was going on. This time, my doctor confronted me with the truth that I had been trying so hard to hide. They found traces of substances in my bloods and wanted to know a few things. How did I manage to get so many tablets, who did I get them from and a lot more. And until I started speaking about it all, there was no way that they were going to let me go anywhere.

So deep down inside, lying there, strapped to a bed covered in piss probably, I made a decision. A decision that scared me to the core yet one that only I could make. This time, no matter how long it took, I would deal with this thing I was fighting. I would end this seemingly never-ending journey somehow and it would be OK. How I was going to do this, at that stage, I did not know, but I was going to do it.

And that's when it began, this long journey out from that dark place, from that place where you feel like you have to hide, from that place where you just want to be yourself but for some unknown reason you feel you can't be. Lying in that bed, looking up at my wife and sister, I knew that I had to do it, if not for me, then for them because I could not carry on like this anymore, I could not carry on hurting them and lying to them even if I did not care a single ounce about myself, I had to do it for someone. And then I looked over, I managed to turn my head slightly to the left and saw those 2 little people and I knew that I had some strength left in me. What right did I have to let my children see me like that, laying there like that? Something changed that day in that dark place and as I started drifting towards that dark place again, my thoughts were on my children. My small children, scared and wondering what was going on.

It can be said that some people spend more time planning their Christmas shopping list than they do sorting out a strategy for their families and relationships, their career and finances but more importantly, for themselves. And this is a real tragedy. People end up reaching a certain time in their life, looking around at where they are and wondering why they are living the life they are with everything seeming so unsatisfying. I am sure that to some extent, you reading this now could be one of those times. It also ends up with people arriving at that time of life called retirement, sadly thinking about the things they would have liked to have done and all the opportunities that they have missed.

As cliché as this may sound, I have some great news. This does not need to be you. And there is no time like now to start creating whatever you choose for your own life. Some of you might cynically think that this is too good to be true and most will be excited at the prospect of what lies ahead. After all, everything you have done thus far has gotten you to where you are now so what is the harm in doing something new? Even better news is the fact that you can even begin to think now of a more exciting life for yourself and this shows that you have the ability to do something about it.

Always remember – it is never too late to start planning or even more so, to start over again! Just to test that it really works, I have done it more than once and it has worked each and every time. As you saw earlier on, I should not be here today, speaking with friends like you, but I am and why? Because what I would love to share with you has the potential to drastically change your life in an amazing way, just like it has done to mine. And even more amazing than that is that you do not have to spend the next however many years of your life making some of the mistakes that I did – this is here for you to use right now.

With a bit of forethought and preparation, you can map out the best possible journey through your own future that lies ahead of you now. Admittedly, and I am not going to lie to you, this will involve some hard and thoroughly enjoyable work, dedication and application, however, it will give you something to live in a way that is rich, full and exciting but more importantly – deeply satisfying.

The second piece of good news is that, in front of you now, you have the foundation you need to start planning anything you choose for yourself.

Seeing as I mentioned foundations there, maybe I could share with you something that I have learnt throughout my career and my life in general. Until recently, I was involved in a profession that my heart was not totally in. I used to go to work every day and wonder why I was doing what I was doing, and how I could possibly help people doing this type of work. For almost 16 years, I worked in the construction industry, both here in England and back home in Zimbabwe. The company I started this profession with trained me from the bottom up – I started there originally to help them computerise things, and gradually as I began to help out around the office, I got drawn into the field of Quantity Surveying.

For those of you that know about construction, we were the ones that everybody did not really enjoy spending time with, basically because of the control that we had over a project. At the start, I was pretty excited to be doing this type of work – it was mentally challenging and you were always learning, and nothing was ever built the same way. Once you had completed a project, you could look back and see that it had all been worthwhile – Clients were happy, suppliers were happy and generally, all around, people got what they had started out for. But not without many challenges along the way.

I thrived upon the challenges that each project brought up because you never knew what was going to happen, yet at the same time, I felt that I was not where I wanted to be. However, for me at that time, a job was a job and that was what people did. Over the years I worked on many different types of building sites and can honestly say that, since coming over here and being involved in the construction industry in a first world country, I have worked on just about every single type of building there is out there. Many years ago, whilst still a little passionate about my job, I set an intention to work on a world renowned project, yet being in Zimbabwe, this seemed rather out of my league. I then achieved that dream and was involved in the construction for Terminal 5 at Heathrow Airport, a building known no matter where you may be in the world. But anyway, having that on your CV in that industry is a pretty big thing. This was when it dawned on me that it was time to take the next step and learn what I needed to learn from all my years doing that job.

Slowly it began to dawn on me the importance of everything that I had been learning.

You see, although some projects may seem to take a lot of time to complete, the time involved in the earlier stages are a lot more significant. Before a building can even go into the ground, there is so much work that is required, without which, NOTHING would ever happen. Schemes have to be designed, drawings have to be done, budgets have to be set, planning permission needs to be granted and so much more.

Even before these things can take place, the Client themselves needs to sit down and decide what he or she would like to do. They need to come up with the concept that can be presented to people who can help them to achieve their dreams. They need to put together a team of qualified people who know what they are doing in order to help them get to where they want to be. They have to then, together, do a lot of groundwork, setting procedures and plans in place, creating partnerships that will be beneficial to all involved and generally making sure that everyone is ready for whatever comes their way.

Once this is done, once plans are approved, once all drawings and schedules are in place and budgets set and agreed, only then can they start digging the ground for possibly the most expensive part of all construction work – the foundation. Without this, nothing goes anywhere. The foundations need to be the sturdiest part of the entire project, they contain the most concrete and steel reinforcement and can also take up quite a lot of time before anything seemingly happens.

Substructure works (as the foundations are commonly known in the industry) also contain a huge amount of risks. Despite the most thorough surveys, you can never fully ascertain what lies below the ground once you start works. You will uncover a number of hidden things that need to be dealt with, and at the same time, also need to be taken into account within budgeting and programming and the like.

And that is when my lesson became clear. For almost 18 years of my life, I had been seeing this put in place every single day, and I had seen the most amazing structures rise out of the ground from churches to hospitals, schools to universities, hotels to clinics and children's homes, roads and bridges and so many more. I had seen old buildings refurbished into amazing new places of employment and enjoyment and acres of empty, abandoned land turned into Old Age Homes, schools and holiday resorts.

But most of all, I had seen how much time and effort had gone into the planning stages to make sure that the end vision was achieved. At first it was rather tiresome and I remember the first time I was involved in a project from start to completion – there were times I never thought it would ever be over. However, I kept going and we got through, refurbishing one of Zimbabwe's top Golf Clubs. And then, I got used to it, I found my feet and it became easier with time. I found that the more effort and concentration I put in at the beginning, the more fun and enjoyment I had as the project went on.

And as I started working on my own life, I found at first that it was pretty tiring to sit down and do all of this planning but I always remembered my old job. If I did not put those strong foundations in place, if I did not put together the right team and prepare for any uncertainty, I would not achieve what I wanted to achieve.

However, even though a solid foundation was required, a building was nothing without the external cladding that made it water tight, safe and sound, as well as look beautiful for the rest of the world to see. Walls had to be built properly before anyone could even consider putting windows and frames and glass into place because without them, they had nothing to hold on to. At the same time, it also took a great amount of work and planning to ensure that this cladding (or facades as the windows are commonly known on tall buildings and the like) was put into place correctly. One millimetre out at the start of a project could have disastrous effects once you got to the top floor.

Once I had gone through this very process that I am about to share with you the first few times, it became second nature to me to take the time out at the beginning. I began to enjoy the process, but more importantly I began to enjoy the construction of my dreams because I knew that I was ready for whatever lay in front of me. I had a team around me that could help me and support me, but again, most importantly, my foundations were strong enough for me to build upon. It was worth the 16 years of studying construction, because it gave me the tools and experience, knowing what is needed to help me achieve what I want to achieve with my life, and thereby being able to help you.

So, switch off your mobile phone, log out of your e-mail, put the "currently away on strategic planning" sign up on your door (I have even made one for you on the next page that you can copy and cut out and hang up) and give yourself a bit of time to make the first step – remember, no more than is required for planning your Christmas shopping list. After all, one of those famous guys many years ago said that the journey of a thousand miles begins with the first step.

DO NOT <u>DISTURB</u>

CURRENTLY AWAY ON STRATEGIC PLANNING

HOW IT WORKS

There has been a lot of research done into the different methods and styles of learning, as well as the retention rates of keeping and applying new information. We do not know the statistics and the figures and can only share here what has worked for us in our lives based on some of the figures that we have seen and monitored ourselves as we tracked our own progress.

These are some of the figures that we came across and that made the most sense based on the level of our personal results, and it is upon this that we created this book.

We learn and retain: -

- **10%** of what we read
- **20%** of what we hear
- **30%** of what we see
- **50%** of what we see and hear – as you listen to someone speak, and make notes, you generally learn and retain more information
- **70%** of what we say – by this, we either mean reading something out loud to yourself, or by repeating what you have heard
- **90%** of what we say and do – by saying it out loud, either by way of affirmations or reading to yourself, as well as

making notes and listening, but then by going out and doing what is suggested, we found that this was when we 1) retained the most information, but more importantly, 2) we had the biggest results and shifts.

As you go through the book you will see that there are pages for you to write things down on. It is our belief that books are living things who enjoy interaction with us as people. We found that when we made notes in our books, either by highlighting relevant points or actually writing down our thoughts, the information stuck and the retention of the information was a lot higher than if we just read. Therefore, we have included many areas in which to make notes as you read, to write down things that you become aware of and just to help you get fully engaged and focused in the process.

All we ask is that you commit to fully engaging in the process, and not just add this book to the list of those that you have read. We dare you to fully engage in the entire process in order to get the best results and we ask that you take on the following 7 Keys to Personal Excellence during the process.

1) Be Flexible. Do something different for a change. Open your mind to other possibilities and options and know that there is always more than one route to get where you want to be.

2) Be Passionate. This is your life and nobody else's. If you cannot be passionate about what you do with your life, then nobody else can or will.

3) Perseverance is KEY. Through this book, you may find some things that challenge you. Keep going and give it everything that you have.

4) Be Committed. Live the life you were born to live and do whatever it takes to live this vision for yourself.

5) Ownership. Take personal responsibility for everything that you do, in an empowering way. If you do not take ownership of your life, then somebody else will; whether you like it or not.

6) Balance. The foundation of life is made up of more than one area. Excel each area of your life – mental, spiritual and physical – and everything else transforms accordingly.

7) Be Prepared. Making mistakes is by far the best way you could ever learn anything, but it is also by far, the best way that you can grow. There is no wrong or right in this life, only what is wrong and right to you and how you deal with the consequences that arise.

As you get to the end of the book, you will find that you now have a very clear and concise action plan. You will have uncovered and dealt with things that have held you back and you will also be ready to achieve some amazing things. As always, we are there to support you along every step of your journey to personal excellence through self discovery and if you have any questions please mail us on book@egoinvenio.com and we will answer them.

All that is left will be for you to take action. Nothing will ever happen if you do not apply what you have created throughout this journey, and there will be some people who do the exercises and then just close the book.

Make the commitment to yourself that you are not one of those people at all. You have already seen that you would like to create an amazing life for yourself so use the tools that you now have available to you in order to go out there and achieve those dreams, no matter what they are.

Now that you have an understanding of how the book is set up, we can give you a brief overview of what you are going to encounter.

Before you go anywhere, we will take a look at a snapshot of where your life is now using a tool that is widely known by many people – that being the Wheel of Life. You will look at each area of your life and decide which one(s) you would like to take the most action on. Some of you may have done this before. However, it is always a good time to take a different look at it.

Together, we will then look into yourself – a foreign place maybe for some people – so that you know what it is that you want from your journey. This will help you to think about your own dreams and maybe narrow them down to the most important ones, yet at the same time gives you a workbook that you can turn to time and time again, just as we do on a regular basis.

We then go on to show you how to set goals (which we will speak about more later) that will empower you to achieve whatever you put your mind to – and for those committed to success in any area of your life that you choose, we believe that our process, combined with your commitment, will lift the lid off your mind and help you to step up to a completely new level to achieve any congruent goal that you set out to attain.

Once you have been through it all, it also gives you a detailed program for you to work on with someone as you have already uncovered information that you can go out and change into more empowering ways of doing things. It also gives you a proven process that you can return to as often as you like – the more you do it, the easier and quicker it gets! Imagine what it was like when you first learnt to walk – it was not that easy to begin with, was it?

We hope you enjoy using this book as much as we have enjoyed putting it together, and we look forward to meeting you along the way.

You begin by **"Digging Deep"** where you will take a look at values and what gives you a sense of meaning in your own life. You will examine the things you find satisfying and the situations where you totally enjoy yourself and time just flies by. Together, we will weigh up your needs and how these could develop in the future.

As only you know what lies in your heart, we begin **"Daring to Dream"** – brainstorming as many things that you can think of that you would like to do, be or have in all areas of your life, preferably in your wildest dreams as well.

However, if you try to achieve all of them at once, you have probably learnt that you don't get nowhere, so in **"A Matter of Choice"** you will narrow these down to get to that core list of things you want to achieve.

Remember, narrowing these down now only means that you achieve those most important to you and when you make them happen, they give you a strong belief to go out there and get the rest done.

In **"Creation"** you now turn these dreams into rich, inspiring visions for your future and set solid goals that will encourage you to achieve them.

Once you have completed the exercises, you will be amazed at how clear your focus becomes and what is more – you will have already taken the first huge step on a well-thought-out strategy towards wonder, happiness and deep inner peace and satisfaction.

So let's take the first step now.

1. WHEEL OF LIFE

Many people have seen, and use on a regular basis, the Wheel of Life. It is a simple Personal Excellence tool that gives you a quick snapshot of your life as you see it when you choose to look at it. It is also a great way to measure each different part of your life to ensure that you are on the right path, and at the same time, to ensure you balance each area of your life with sufficient focus.

Think of your life as a see-saw – you need to balance each area so that it does not topple over. I remember there was time where my career was soaring and my finances were on the up, however, the relationships around me were falling to pieces. It was when this tool was introduced to me that I realised I needed to balance all areas of my life instead of just focusing on one or 2 areas only.

In the diagram that follows, you will see a blank Wheel of Life that we personally use for our own lives as well as with people that work with. Further on, we will explain each area in a bit more detail. You will then give yourself a mark out of 10 on each of the spokes of the wheel. To get an accurate snapshot, you are going to need to be honest as the more honest you are, the easier it will be to chart your own progress.

Don't imagine how you would like things to be in this first exercise – take them as they are.

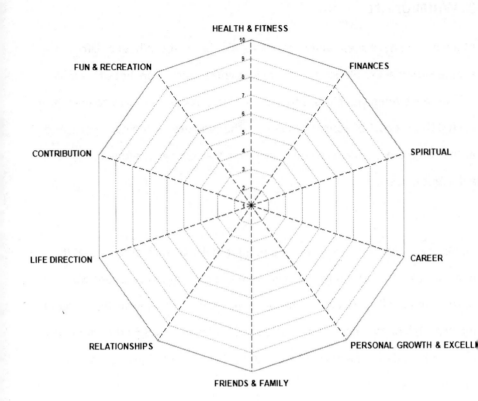

1.1 HEALTH & FITNESS

Are you the type of person who exercises regularly and feels vibrant and full of energy whilst everyone around you is feeling tired and getting all sorts of bugs and illnesses?

Do you eat healthily and ensure that you drink good amounts of water and the like?

When you see yourself in the mirror are you happy with what you see and do you get comments from people about how healthy and well you look?

If this is the type of person that you are and you take care of and look after yourself well, then your score would be a 10 on the wheel.

On the reverse side of the coin, maybe you open your eyes in the morning and the thought of getting out of bed does not exactly excite you. Instead of starting the day with breakfast, you maybe get a quick coffee on the way to work with the thought that you can always make up for it at lunch time. All of a sudden, the day has passed and you have forgotten about that lunch and it is almost time to leave for the day. You get home and quickly throw something into the microwave while making a mental note that tomorrow you need to do some sort of shopping for "supplies" rather than groceries. You flick on the TV and fall asleep on the couch, or maybe, rather than doing all of this, you are making your way home from the pub after a few too many with mates where you all laughed and joked about some comment to do with thinking about going for a jog and wondering if you were catching that nasty flu bug that was going around?

Now that may seem a bit drastic, or does it really? But if that sounds like someone you know quite well then you would score around a 2 or 3 on the wheel.

Fortunately, you are here reading this so that means you won't be quite as low as a 1 and you may also have some sort of plan in place which means you could score a little higher up.

Nevertheless, take an honest look at your own Health and Fitness and give yourself an honest mark of how your life is now.

1.2 FINANCES

Before we talk about this, it is one thing to remember that it is not about the amount of money that you have in your own life and we are sure that you have heard this before so we will not go into that. It is more about your relationship with your own personal finances.

Someone could be earning vast amounts of money due to investments and career and the like, however, their spending habits leave a lot to be desired. They constantly have to dip into savings and skip paying the bills because their focus is on other things. Some people refer to this as having more month at the end of the money and it is not a great place to be in.

Or maybe you are the kind of person that thinks very carefully about the way you use your own money. You know exactly what you are going to do with it each month, ensuring that all bills are paid on time and even have a savings plan for those emergencies and treats in life. You know that money comes in and goes out and you have a good knowledge of exactly where you stand at any time.

It is common knowledge with all of us that money is definitely not the most important thing in our lives, however, many of those things close and dear to us are made a lot easier by the management of our own money. This is the vital difference in this area. No matter which way you look at it, give yourself an honest score on this area of your life.

1.3 SPIRITUAL

Regardless of what you believe in and what faith you hold close to your heart, do you stand strong and true to your values and the way that you live your life so that when people speak about you, they can say what you stand for?

If you are able to find peace and contentment when all others around you are losing their heads and you feel a strong connection to that which is your source, then you probably would rate quite high in this area of your life?

Or maybe, you constantly question everything that goes on around you. You wonder why all these things only happen to you and ask yourself why you feel so alone and disconnected from everything and everyone. You know that there could be more out there but you just are not sure which path to follow and which one is right for you.

No matter where you are, take a look at your life as it is and give yourself a score.

1.4 CAREER

It has been said that if you do what you love, you will never have to work a day in your life, and to some people, that may seem somewhat crazy – how can I be in a 9 to 5 job, stuck in an office and working from pay day to pay day.

Which side of this equation are you on?

No matter what you do for a living, do you wake up in the morning with a spring in your step, ready to take on another day and everything that it brings with it?

Do you walk into your office with a smile on your face, greet the people that you work with and bring a good "vibe" to the office?

Or do you turn over when the alarm goes off, hit the snooze button and pray for just another hour in bed before you have to face the day again, wondering when the next weekend is going to come around?

Rate yourself in this area of your life, based on where it is right now.

1.5 PERSONAL GROWTH AND EXCELLENCE

Word has just got out that Richard Branson, or someone that you aspire to, has just released their latest book on how they grew to become the person that they are now. You get excited at the thought of finding out what the difference was that made them get ahead.

Or maybe you heard some friends talking about something that you did not know about before and you felt that it could help you in your life. So you go out and look into it. Do you like to learn and grow or have a strong need for development in your life? Do you strive to become a better person and want to step up in your life and be somebody?

If that is the case, then you score highly in this area. Growth and excellence in your life is important to you and what you stand for, and the fact that you are reading this shows that this area is vital to all that you do, so well done for that.

If you can't remember the last time you read a non-fiction book or maybe this is the first time that you have come across the Wheel of Life because a friend passed this on to you. Have you ever invested your time and resources into working on yourself rather than something else, taking a look at your life and how you can improve things?

Or maybe you have just begun to realise now that there is so much more to life and all that you can do so things are slowly beginning to change.

If so, then welcome to the world of Personal Growth and Excellence – you are going to love it.

Give yourself an honest mark as it stands right now, not as you would like it to be.

1.6 FRIENDS & FAMILY

Some people go by the saying that sounds something like "we can't choose our families but we can choose our friends." I would go on to add to that and say that whilst we cannot choose our families, we ourselves have the power within us now to be the type of person that brings a family together. How do you get on with your closest family – your parents, brothers, sisters, spouses, partners, and children?

Do you have the kind of family where everybody really cares about each other and you are all concerned for each other's wellbeing and needs? You have fun together, speak regularly if you do not live in the same home and are there to support one another during the rough patches that life throws our way, knowing that together as a family, you can pull through things.

Are you the type of person that has taken advantage of creating a perfect family for yourself maybe, and calling them friends? You watch that old series on television with the aptly titled name and can really relate to how they are all there for each other, knowing what is going on and ready to lend a listening ear in times of need but at the same time, having loads of fun.

If this is you and the quality of your friends and family is something very dear to you, then you would score high in this area of your life.

Or maybe you don't remember when the last time was that you spoke to your brother or sister and know that you should call them, but just once you finish off doing the stuff that you are doing now. Or perhaps the thought of the upcoming family function is making you really nervous, wondering what is going to happen next.

Another weekend arrives and the thought of sitting home alone again really makes you quite depressed. You have sent out a few messages and emails and everyone seems to be busy again. And the people that have responded are the ones that really make you feel uncomfortable and irritated so you would rather stay at home anyway. It may sound strange to some, but there are people out there who are constantly changing their circle of friends because so-and-so does this to upset them and the other one is just so boring.

If that is the case, or maybe right now, it is not that bad, then your score in this area of your life would be quite low. Where do you honestly sit on the scale now?

Go ahead and rate yourself.

1.7 RELATIONSHIPS

Everyone is involved in relationships of many different sorts – be it those that you work with, those that you encounter on a daily basis, or those of the romantic kind.

How do you show up each and every day in the relationships that you have – what kind of friend are you or what is it like working with you? How do you relate to your partner or significant other? Is the relationship going well or does it have moments where you wish you could be somewhere else, doing something else with someone else? You could have been single for a while, or just not found that right person, and are constantly wondering why everyone else around you is so happy.

If you were outside the room, what would those people say about you? How would they describe you and the relationship you have with them? If they were organising a party, would you be the one person that they could choose to have there because of the way you get on with people, or would they be thinking that it would be best to keep quiet about the whole thing just in case you found out.

Look at the quality of the relationships that you have in your life right now and give yourself a score in this area.

1.8 LIFE DIRECTION

You regularly take time out to work on what you want in the future, creating vision boards and the like so that you know you are on course. You see yourself doing things that make your heart sing and you get excited at the way things are working out, no matter what happens, because you know that you are on course for an amazing destiny.

You have a plan for the next 1, 3, 5 and 10 years and are taking active, enjoyable steps towards this. You live your life with passion and enthusiasm and others are drawn along with you, enjoying the time spent as well.

Or possibly, you aren't quite sure what you are even going to do after work or this coming weekend and you think "how on earth could I think about what I want to be doing in 5 years time when I don't even know what is going on right now?"

Thoughts of the future, and all that it holds, overwhelm you and so many things seem beyond your control and you find yourself feeling rather unsatisfied with life yet think at the same time that this is how it should be really.

Give yourself a mark for where you currently stand with your own life and the direction that it is taking and the direction that you would like it to take.

1.9 CONTRIBUTION

Many people think that contribution means donating financially to causes outside of themselves, and whilst this could be a part of it, it is not necessarily the sole way of giving back. It is also about giving your time, your resources, your energy and spirit to things without wanting or needing anything in return for it.

When last did you help out in your community in any way or give someone a hand with a task that seemed overwhelming to them? Have you ever given up some of your time to go and spend the day at a children's home or an old age home? Or do you contribute to ways that will improve your society in general?

Or maybe you spend quite a bit of time complaining about how things are not they way that they used to be and how things are changing and how things are so untidy and unruly right now? You have the line of thought that you have done enough for others so maybe it is time that someone did something for you? Now I know that that may sound a little drastic, but you get the picture, right?

How do you give back and contribute to a greater cause, no matter what it is? Your honest score will indicate where this area of your life is at right now.

1.10 FUN & RECREATION

How you spend your spare time is vital to creating a balanced life filled with fun and exciting times, as well as regular rest and refreshment.

You love visiting new places or going out to different functions to experience different ways of life. There is a lot of laughter in your life and you can remember the last time that you acted like a child and maybe jumped in a puddle or ran through the fallen leaves on the ground. The thought of your next holiday fills you with excitement as your start planning it and you take time out to enjoy the simple pleasures in your life, no matter what they are – just because you can!

Or possibly, the thought of going out to the movies and for dinner makes you seriously question the amount of money that you could be using on something else?

Seeing people "playing the fool" is something that possibly makes you slightly uncomfortable and the thought of taking on a new challenge such as a dance class or speed dating is rather immature.

Everyone has their own idea of having fun, but are you really having fun in your life? Where do you sit right now – give yourself a score to see where you stand.

1.11 WRAPPING IT ALL UP!

Now that wasn't as bad as you thought it would be, was it?

Some people may never have looked at all the areas of their life as they have just done and it may have made them slightly uncomfortable because it has uncovered a few truths. If that is the case, then that is really great because it shows that you are open to improving things and getting that balance and freedom back in your life.

But more importantly, what it does is give you a snapshot of where everything is standing right now, and again, how you can get some balance back. If you have been subconsciously focusing on one aspect of your life, you may find that the other areas are falling lower and this is a good way to see that.

It also shows you which areas you can improve upon to make your life even more exciting.

Before we go ahead, the next step you need to take is join up all those different scores so that you have something that looks like the diagram on the next page. Once you have done this, imagine for a minute if you would, that this was the wheel that has been driving your life up to this point.

Does the shape you have created give you an even wheel because there are very few people who have that type of shape?

Or like the one shown below, do you have one that is very pointy and irregular because that is not a bad thing at all. In fact, it is a very good thing as it highlights exactly where you need to put some temporary focus in order to get things back in balance.

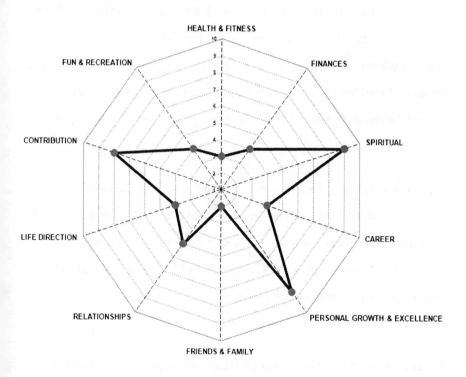

This is in fact one of the Wheel's of Life that I (Gareth) did for myself not too long ago when I made the decision to change careers and start following my true passion, which I had uncovered using the steps we will go through.

Because of what I had been through, I realised that I had been working so hard on my own personal growth and excellence, as well as repairing my own spiritual relationship with my faith, I did not realise that in the process, the other areas in my life were suffering quite badly.

I looked at my own wheel and saw that it was no wonder things were so bumpy all the time because I did not have that balance that I needed in order to have a smoother ride. It was at that stage as well that I realised that, even though I was enjoying my work and doing well in my career, it was not where I wanted my life to be going. In other words, it highlighted an area of my life that could have caused me huge problems later on had I carried on the way that I had been and for that, I was extremely grateful.

And I guess now it is clear to see how vital it is to have that strong foundation in place. It is almost impossible to work solely on one area of your life without it having an adverse effect on every other area. A rise in one area, combined with a solid foundation, is all that it takes to slowly begin lifting every other score you have.

It was an extremely good snapshot of everything going on and once I had seen this on paper, I realised what areas I needed to work on in order to bring back that kind of balance.

So now that you have completed your Wheel of Life, joined up the points and seen how things are going for you, take a look at your shape. For the purpose of the rest of this book, choose the areas of your life that you think require raising the score to a higher one.

As you work through the exercises that follow, use these areas to start with. You can always come back later on for the remaining ones.

It is those with the lower scores that need your current attention in order to give you a balanced and health life and lifestyle.

2. DIGGING DEEP

DIGGING DEEP

DARING TO DREAM

A MATTER OF CHOICE

CREATION

The first thing we need to do before we go anywhere is to take a look at what is going on inside and this is vital if you are going to live your life in a way that is completely consistent with who you are and who you want to become. For some this may be the first time they have ever taken a look there.

It is not always that simple to pin point exactly what is most important to you or to establish the things that make you satisfied and fulfilled but it is worth making the effort to do this so that you can make sure that the life you choose is one that will bring lasting happiness to you.

Whilst giving you a good foundation and starting point, it also gives you something that you can come back to as you refine your dreams to make sure that the ones you have chosen to begin with now will give you the happiness that you desire.

It also gives you a very good ground from which to mind map (or brain storm) the many strategies that you could follow from here on forward.

There are a number of ways that we could go about this step of the journey. To begin with, we will take a look at some of the times where you have been at your happiest. Times when you have looked on in pride at the work that you have achieved and finally, at times when you have really thought that your life has had meaning.

From there, we will move on to take a look at your values, those attributes that you hold close and dear. This will help you to make sure the journey you take is consistent and aligned with values that you consider to be important. Very often, the results we have in our life today are a reflection of our top values. Taking a look at these can make a significant difference in your progress from this point onwards.

To close off this section, you will take a look at your needs – this establishes any areas of your life where your needs are not being met and makes sure that the chosen strategy addresses those needs.

As daunting as this may sound, this section may take some people longer than others, however, the important thing to remember is that there is no right or wrong; there is only what feels right for you. Some parts may appear easier than others. Remember, this can be re-visited again and again. The vital thing to remember is to start now. Once you commit to the process you may find yourself pleasantly surprised.

2.1 UNDERSTANDING YOU

Before going any further, we would like to explain something that some people may already know which would be good to go over again in a different light.

For others, it could be the first time they have come across this and it makes things easier to understand as we progress.

It can be said that nothing in our lives has the meaning except the meaning that we actually give it. It is the way that we process the information that comes to us that makes us do the things that we do and therefore, get the results that we get out of life. Regardless of what we want or whether we like it or not.

Look at it this way.

I am wearing red sunglasses and you have a pair of blue sunglasses on yourself. A friend of ours comes along and they are wearing, say, yellow ones. We are sitting and talking and a man in a white suit walks along.

Now we all know that white is white, but with our sunglasses on, it takes on a different colour or shade.

Until each of us realises that our sunglasses are filtering things in our own world, we will never be able to look at the suit in the same way. This unique meaning that we ascribe to something would then affect the way we feel inside. Subsequently, our behaviour and our results are affected. We could argue all day long about the colour or shade of the white suit because no matter how we look at it, the way we are processing the information is different, so therefore, so are all of our results.

These "sunglasses" can be looked at as our values and beliefs, the things that we hold close and dear to ourselves. Either through the way we have been brought up or conditioned by our societies, or by the choices that we have made in the past in our lives. They are the way we live day to day because it is what we know. Once we accept this process, it is then that we can start shaping our own future, and thereby the results that we get in all areas.

Let's say that you are working on relationships right now.

What "sunglasses" are you currently wearing that are affecting the results that you are getting?

You can only get the results that you know or have learnt and again, once you accept this and understand it, then you are well on the way to changing things.

On a deeper level (and one that a lot of people are very passionate about) it can be referred to as Quantum Reality or the fact that our internal world and representation directly affects the external world that we live in, and again, the results that we get for ourselves.

Our internal "sunglasses" will determine everything that we experience because they are what we use to look at the world.

However, some of these things were put in place long ago without us maybe even knowing about them due to what we could have been through at a young age. We then begin to assume that the way we look at things is the way that the world actually is.

This could be covered in so much more detail, but for the purpose of what we are working on here, it covers the basics of it. With a bit of time and thought, as we go through things along the way, it will make a lot of sense.

Can you honestly say that you know what makes you feel happy?

What gives you a sense of meaning in your own life or what fills you with pride?

Identifying situations where you have felt these things before and then discovering what elements contributed to this is like opening the hood of a car and seeing how the engine runs.

Should you struggle to find things like this in your life try and imagine what colour sunglasses someone else (who you feel is in a better situation at the moment or is in a position you would like to be in) would wear?

How would they look out at the world or this area of their lives?

2.1.1 What Makes You Happy?

Based on the areas of your life that you have chosen to excel on, identify times in which you have been particularly happy - times when you have felt very content and at peace with what you have been doing.

Recall everything in as much detail as you can – remember the things you saw and heard, what about them made you feel happy? How did they specifically make you happy and what did that mean to you?

Maybe you have a particular hobby that you like and when you sit down and do this, the time just seems to disappear. Many years ago, I used to dance competitively with my sister and prior to competitions, we used to train for hours on end. It was extremely tiring but when we stepped out on to the dance floor on the night of a competition, despite the nerves, there was a deep sense of happiness as we both loved to dance.

Or I remember a time when my children were small and we were playing outside in the garden, running through the sprinkler that was watering the lawn. I remember them giggling and screaming like little kids do and I clearly recall that feeling of happiness coming from deep down inside.

For each of these situations, write down the factors that have contributed to making these times happy ones.

Taking a look at a few different areas may help to give you a spectrum of ideas that contribute to your happiness and you may be able to see a pattern or theme surrounding these cases, however, if you feel more comfortable looking at it in only one or two areas, there is nothing wrong with this.

HAPPY TIME No. 1

Contributing Factors: -

1.

2.

3.

4.

5.

6.

HAPPY TIME No. 2

Contributing Factors: -

1.	2.
3.	4.
5.	6.

HAPPY TIME No. 3

Contributing Factors: -

1.	2.
3.	4.
5.	6.

HAPPY TIME No. 4

Contributing Factors: -

1.	2.
3.	4.
5.	6.

HAPPY TIME No. 5

Contributing Factors: -

1.

2.

3.

4.

5.

6.

Having completed this, re-visit each one and identify the **five factors that are most important to you.**

At the end of this section, you will find a summary sheet for you to record these top 5 points. Under the **"Happy"** section in this summary, write them down.

2.1.2 WHAT MAKES YOU PROUD?

Now that you have the hang of it, we are going to take a look (following the same process for happiness) at situations in which you have felt particularly proud of your achievements and the work or results that you got in your life.

Again, recall those situations in as much detail as you can. The more effort you put into the process, the greater the results that you will get. Get that feeling of pride coursing through your body so that it feels like you are right back in that time and place, really re-living the moment.

Imagine someone that you look up to in a situation that they were proud of. How would they feel and act? How would they stand and hold themselves? What would they be saying to themselves internally?

PRIDE SITUATION No. 1

Contributing Factors: -

1.	2.
3.	4.
5.	6.

PRIDE SITUATION No. 2

Contributing Factors: -

1.	2.
3.	4.
5.	6.

PRIDE SITUATION No. 3

Contributing Factors: -

1.

2.

3.

4.

5.

6.

PRIDE SITUATION No. 4

Contributing Factors: -

1.	2.
3.	4.
5.	6.

PRIDE SITUATION No. 5

Contributing Factors: -

1.	2.
3.	4.
5.	6.

Again, having completed this, re-visit each one and identify the **five factors that are most important to you.**

On your summary sheet under the "Proud" section, write down these top five factors.

2.1.3 WHAT FULFILS YOU?

Now, we are going to take a look at the situations in your life when you have felt a real sense of fulfilment and meaning.

Maybe there was a time in the past where, without even thinking twice, you reached out and helped somebody in a time of great need and were a huge source of strength for them. Or you took some time out to volunteer for a charity close to your heart.

For some, this may appear difficult, however, as you look back now, write down those times that come easily to your mind.

Once again, identify up to five situations looking at the factors that gave you these feelings of deep meaning and fulfilment.

FULFILMENT AND MEANING No. 1

Contributing Factors: -

1.

2.

3.

4.

5.

6.

FULFILMENT AND MEANING No. 2

Contributing Factors: -

1.	2.
3.	4.
5.	6.

FULFILMENT AND MEANING No. 3

Contributing Factors: -

1.	2.
3.	4.
5.	6.

FULFILMENT AND MEANING No. 4

Contributing Factors: -

1.	2.
3.	4.
5.	6.

FULFILMENT AND MEANING No. 5

Contributing Factors: -

1.	2.
3.	4.
5.	6.

Finally, re-visit them and identify the **five factors that are most important to you.**

Again, under the "Fulfilment and Meaning" section in your summary sheet, write them down.

2.2 VALUE FINDING

Next up on the journey into you, we are going to take a look at your values.

Values are ideals, beliefs, morals, characteristics or traits that keep you true to your path and true to yourself. You plot your journey through life based on that which you believe to be true, your ethics and what is most important to you. The hierarchy of your values will often determine the destination towards which you are going, or in other words, your priority of values determines the results you achieve.

As you can see, they are powerful things to focus on in your life.

If you are going against your values in the way that you live and work, it is highly likely that you will feel uncomfortable or "out of place" with what you are doing, sometimes even very unhappy.

On the flip side of the coin, when you are working in a way that is aligned with your values, you are far more likely to be happy and satisfied.

An interesting aspect of working with values is that different people can have very totally different value systems and beliefs, yet still feel complete happiness.

This also explains why your dreams and choices in life can quite often be radically different to those of the person working next to you or living next door. It is also why it is vital to plot your own strategy in life and not mimic those of other people – even if those other people are loving family members who only want the best for you.

So now, let us find out what your core values in your life are!

STEP 1

Start off by looking at the things from the previous section – those that made you happy, proud and fulfilled with a sense of meaning (you can also take a look at your summary sheet.)

Identify any values that you think may emerge from this list and write them down on the table below: -

POSSIBLE VALUES I COULD HAVE: -	
1.	2.
3.	4.
5.	6.
7.	8.

STEP 2

On the following pages, we have listed some more values that people have indicated as being important in the way they work and live their lives.

Again, values can be defined as the beliefs or ideals that a person holds in which they have some sort of emotional investment or attachment to. They influence the decisions that we as well as the results and level of success that we achieve.

They can also cause internal conflict within us when our behaviour, or the behaviour of others', goes against them. They arise as a result of the experiences that we have in life and are also influenced by many different things – our family and friends, media and society, religion and geography. All these have a significant impact in what we hold true to ourselves as our own personal values. And at the same time, they are "installed" from a very young age as well.

A large section of this book could be dedicated to this subject – how they are formed, where they come from, why they are important and the like. However, we just want to give you a brief introduction and hope that this gives you an insight into what we believe they are. Think back to near the beginning of the book when we spoke about the sunglasses – a very similar approach applies here to how we live and the results that we create.

For the purpose of this exercise, we are going to look at over-riding values that we live our lives by. It is possible that we can have a certain set of values that influence our relationships yet at the same time, we can also value different things when it comes to how we run a business or how we play sport.

All of them are important to some people in some situations, but which ones do you feel may be important to you?

You may not need to write down any further values as you may have already covered them above. Sometimes just taking a look at others helps us put into words something that we could not quite uncover previously.

Accountability	Discipline	Humility	Results-orientated
Accuracy	Discretion	Independence	Security
Achievement	Diversity	Ingenuity	Self Control
Adventure	Dynamism	Inner Harmony	Selflessness
Altruism	Effectiveness	Inquisitiveness	Self Reliance
Ambition	Efficiency	Intelligence	Sensitivity
Assertiveness	Elegance	Intellectual	Serenity
Balance	Empathy	Status	Service
Being the best	Enjoyment	Intuition	Shrewdness
Belonging	Enthusiasm	Irreverence	Simplicity
Boldness	Equality	Joy	Soundness
Calmness	Excellence	Justice	Speed
Carefulness	Excitement	Leadership	Spontaneity
Challenge	Expertise	Legacy	Stability
Clear-mindedness	Exploration	Love	Strategic
Commitment	Expression	Loyalty	Strength
Community	Fairness	Making a	Structure
Compassion	Faith	Difference	Success
Competitiveness	Family	Mastery	Support
Consistency	Fidelity	Merit	Teamwork
Contentment	Fluency	Obedience	Temperance
Continuous	Focus	Openness	Thankfulness
Improvement	Freedom	Optimism	Thoroughness
Contribution	Fun	Order	Thoughtfulness
Control	Generosity	Originality	Timeliness
Cooperation	Goodness	Patriotism	Tolerance
Correctness	Grace	Perfection	Trust
Courtesy	Growth	Persistence	Truth-seeking
Creativity	Happiness	Philanthropy	Understanding
Curiosity	Hard Work	Positivity	Uniqueness
Decisiveness	Health	Practicality	Unity
Democracy	Helping	Professionalism	Usefulness
Dependability	Others	Prudence	Vision
Determination	Holiness	Quality	Vigour
Devoutness	Honesty	Reliability	Vitality
Diligence	Honour	Resourcefulness	
		Restraint	

ADDITIONAL VALUES I COULD HAVE: -

1.	2.
3.	4.
5.	6.
7.	8.

Now taking a look at both the **"possible values"** and the **"additional values"** that you may have identified as being vitally important in the way that you live your life, **select the top five.**

On the summary sheet, put these in under the **"My Top 5 Values"** section.

2.3 WHAT I NEED

As your values are likely to be different to other people's, in the same way so are your needs. Here, we are looking at a need as something that is essential to your personal sense of well-being and that which inspires and motivates you to take some sort of action to meet.

If we take a look at the bigger picture of our existence, the needs we each have as a person are very similar, and some of you may be familiar with Maslow's Hierarchy of Needs.

This states that people attend to their needs in a certain order beginning with basic physiological needs, moving on to a sense security, a feeling of being part of something, a need for self worth. Finally a need for being all or everything that we can possible be.

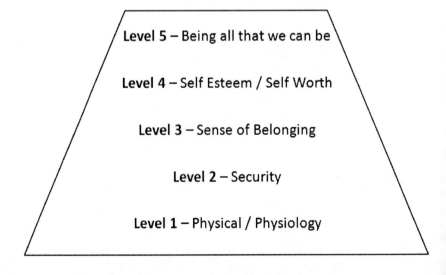

Level 5 – Being all that we can be

Level 4 – Self Esteem / Self Worth

Level 3 – Sense of Belonging

Level 2 – Security

Level 1 – Physical / Physiology

As part of this process, we are going to assume that you are satisfying the relevant needs explained in the first 2 levels above. In other words, that you have enough to eat and drink, you have sufficient shelter and that you are relatively healthy and secure in your life.

If this is not the case, as a matter of priority we would suggest that you attend to these needs now.

However, when we take a look at the remaining levels – 3, 4 and 5 – are your needs being met there? We need to look at the needs you can have at these levels so that you can establish whether they are being met or not.

Listed below are some of the common needs that people tend to have on these levels. Take a look through them and as you do, think of the people that are around you because you will be able to identify some who may clearly need some of these things as well as others who have different ones. And just as others have needs that are evident to them, so do you.

Again take a look at this list and circle those that most affect you regardless of whether they are already met or unmet. It must be noted that you need to take care not to underestimate the importance of the needs that you have already met because you will want to ensure that they are met in the future too. And again, if an important need of yours is missing from this list, write it down and circle it.

Accomplishment	Family	Mastery	Respect
Acceptance	Fairness	Morality	Responsibility
Adventure	Freedom	Opportunity	Safety
Authority	Friendship	Order	Security
Balance	Honesty	Organisation	Self Esteem
Belonging	Humour	Peace	Service
Clarity	Influence	Participation	Significance
Competence	Justice	Passion	Spirituality
Connection	Knowledge	Pleasure	Trust
Control	Kindness	Power	Variety
Discipline	Love	Quiet	Value
Duty	Loyalty	Recognition	

Once you have circled those that you feel apply to your life, identify the **top five needs that are most important to you**, and again, on the **"My Top 5 Needs"** section in your summary sheet, write these down.

2.4 PULLING IT TOGETHER

So, you have got this far and it has not been that bad, so well done to you.

This is more than most people would do in a lifetime and for this you should congratulate yourself.

As you can see from your Summary, you now have a pretty good understanding of the things that make you happy, proud and fulfilled.

You also understand the values that you want to bring into your strategy for your life and the personal needs that must be met for you to have an excellent journey into future.

THIS IS VITAL – not only are they an extremely powerful foundation upon which to begin your journey of personal excellence through self discovery, they also help you make choices and then plan your dreams in such a way that brings you success, happiness and ultimately, fulfilment and a deep sense of satisfaction.

LOOKING INSIDE – SUMMARY SHEET

Based on the work that you have completed above, transfer the relevant top five factors for each situation into the table below. These will be used as we go on through the rest of the book.

WHAT MAKES ME HAPPY: -

1._____
2._____
3._____
4._____
5._____

WHAT MAKES ME PROUD: -

1._____
2._____
3._____
4._____
5._____

WHAT GIVES ME FULFILMENT AND MEANING: -

1._____
2._____
3._____
4._____
5._____

MY TOP FIVE VALUES: -

1._____

2._____

3._____

4._____

5._____

MY TOP FIVE NEEDS: -

1._____

2._____

3._____

4._____

5._____

3. DARING TO DREAM

```
┌─────────────────┐
│    DIGGING      │
│     DEEP        │
└─────────────────┘
```

Now that we have got the hard work out of the way, it is time to relax a bit and have some fun, so let's get started on those dreams of yours.

```
┌─────────────────┐
│   DARING TO     │
│    DREAM        │
└─────────────────┘
```

Take a few moments to reflect on all the dreams you may have had about your future and how that might be. Different dreams at different stages of your life. Looking ahead towards different, perfect situations somewhere out there now.

```
┌─────────────────┐
│   A MATTER OF   │
│    CHOICE       │
└─────────────────┘
```

```
┌─────────────────┐
│                 │
│    CREATION     │
│                 │
└─────────────────┘
```

Now is the time to bring them all together and to dream some more.

Over the page is a table – don't look yet – and what you can do is write down some things from the following. Remember, there is no wrong or right !

- **What you would like to DO in the future** – these can be things that you would love to do with your career. Sports that you would like to have a go at. Activities that you would like to do to help other people or qualifications that you would like to get for yourself

- **What would you like to BE in the future** – maybe you want to be an explorer or traveller, an excellent parent or partner, a dynamic leader in your community or even CEO of your own company, the choice is yours.

- **Where you would like to GO in the future** – maybe you have always wanted to travel to far off places around the world or go swimming with dolphins. There may even be a certain cruise that you would like to go on?

- **What would you like to HAVE** – is there a vehicle that you have always had your eye on or a particular watch, computer or piece of jewellery that has caught your eye on a number of occasions ?

For some, this may seem like a futile exercise but, for someone like you who is committed to a life of excellence, this is an exciting exercise to do. Just let your mind run wild and write down **at least 100 dreams** that you have for your life in the space provided. Your aim here is to get everything you have ever wanted out of your head and onto paper.

Some of them may seem small and some of them will seem big – but more importantly, dream and get it all out because if your mind can imagine it, then it is within your realm of possibility no matter how extravagant it may appear.

If you do get stuck, or become fixated on a particular type of dream, ensure that you cover dreams in all areas of your life and not just the ones in the areas of your life that you would like to improve – the categories are shown again below for you: -

Personal Growth and Excellence

Fun and Recreation

Friends and Family

Life Direction

Career

Relationships

Contribution

Health and Fitness

Finances

Spiritual

Focusing on all the areas of your life gives you good direction in preparing a strategy for the successful accomplishment of your dreams and goals rather than just focusing on a few that may be at the forefront of your mind.

Also remember the work that you have already completed in the last section – look back over the lists that you wrote out in your summary sheets and think what sort of positions, situations or things might help you to relive these feelings – be like a kid in a candy shop because your own life is yours to create and claim.

Let your imagination have some fun as you do this exercise and included all the things that come to your mind.

MY TOP 100 DREAMS AND ASPIRATIONS, GOALS AND DESIRES

1.

2.

3.

4.

5.

6.

7.

8.

9.

10.

11.

12.

13.

14.

15.

MY TOP 100 DREAMS AND ASPIRATIONS, GOALS AND DESIRES

16.

17.

18.

19.

20.

21.

22.

23.

24.

25.

26.

27.

28.

29.

30.

MY TOP 100 DREAMS AND ASPIRATIONS, GOALS AND DESIRES

31.

32.

33.

34.

35.

36.

37.

38.

39.

40.

41.

42.

43.

44.

45.

MY TOP 100 DREAMS AND ASPIRATIONS, GOALS AND DESIRES

46.

47.

48.

49.

50.

51.

52.

53.

54.

55.

56.

57.

58.

59.

60.

MY TOP 100 DREAMS AND ASPIRATIONS, GOALS AND DESIRES

61.

62.

63.

64.

65.

66.

67.

68.

69.

70.

71.

72.

73.

74.

75.

MY TOP 100 DREAMS AND ASPIRATIONS, GOALS AND DESIRES

76.

77.

78.

79.

80.

81.

82.

83.

84.

85.

86.

87.

88.

89.

90.

MY TOP 100 DREAMS AND ASPIRATIONS, GOALS AND DESIRES

91.	
92.	
93.	
94.	
95.	
96.	
97.	
98.	
99.	
100.	

If you have not written down 100 dream and aspirations, revisit your summary sheets and use these as staring points for thinking about what you could and might do.

Again, make sure you cover all of the points mentioned.

If you have filled up all of these pages and you still have yet to complete writing down all that you want to do, then congratulations to you! Just keep writing on a separate piece of paper at a later stage and continue on to the next section.

In order to go forward in our lives, we need to find that compelling reason and create what some people call leverage for ourselves. When we have that compelling reason as to why we should do things, we find that all of a sudden, things become more apparent or clear to us. We understand why we need to improve or change certain things and we find it easier to move forwards.

This may seem rather futile for now, given that we have just got ourselves all excited, but we found that getting excited about our future was not enough. It let us down in the past and we used to wonder why. That was when we came across this exercise and began doing it more and more.

These may prove quite challenging, however once you push through the barrier that you feel could be holding you back, it becomes a lot simpler. As always, we are only going to be honest with you and we do not want to sit here and say "wow, this is simple" because it will cause a bit of discomfort that will be far outweighed by the results you begin to achieve now once you have completed it.

To start off with this second part, we are going to list down how your life will not be if you do not go out there and achieve these goals for yourself.

It may seem a little negative right now but please trust us on this one.

How is your life not going to be if you do not improve the quality of your relationships, or how is your life not going to be if you do not get all the things that you have just spent time and effort writing down?

How would it make you feel if you did absolutely NONE of them?

Take some time and write down 50 of these, and make sure you complete them all.

How will not doing these things make you feel?

HOW WILL MY LIFE NOT BE WHEN I DON'T ACHIEVE THESE THINGS?

1.

2.

3.

4.

5.

6.

7.

8.

9.

10.

11.

12.

13.

14.

15

HOW WILL MY LIFE NOT BE WHEN I DON'T ACHIEVE THESE THINGS?

16.

17.

18.

19.

20.

21.

22.

23.

24.

25.

26.

27.

28.

29.

30.

HOW WILL MY LIFE NOT BE WHEN I DON'T ACHIEVE THESE THINGS?

31.

32.

33.

34.

35.

36.

37.

38.

39.

40.

41.

42.

43.

44.

45.

HOW WILL MY LIFE NOT BE WHEN I DON'T ACHIEVE THESE THINGS?

46.

47.

48.

49.

50.

Excellent and well done for getting through that!

The great news is that the next one is going to be a lot easier than this.

You have now created a written testament as to the things you do not want showing up in your life.

Now, based on the work that we have done with your values and your needs, we are going to create the list of compelling reasons for you to take action now. This is also going to help you a great deal when you get to the final part of the process and begin setting your goals for yourself.

Remember that the bulk of the work is *ALWAYS IN THE FOUNDATION*. They are what keep those tall buildings strong during tough weather, and the time that you have spent so far on your own foundations is going to give you huge results as you start constructing the rest of whatever it is that you are going to build.

In the table below, go ahead and write 50 reasons WHY you should do and have these things?

Why do you need them? Why do the people around you deserve them?

Will they make you a better colleague?

Will they improve your health and give you more vitality and energy?

Will they bring you the freedom you crave?

WHY SHOULD I DO AND HAVE THESE THINGS IN MY LIFE?

1.

2.

3.

4.

5.

6.

7.

8.

9.

10.

11.

12.

13.

14.

15

WHY SHOULD I DO AND HAVE THESE THINGS IN MY LIFE?

16.

17.

18.

19.

20.

21.

22.

23.

24.

25.

26.

27.

28.

29.

30.

WHY SHOULD I DO AND HAVE THESE THINGS IN MY LIFE?

31.

32.

33.

34.

35.

36.

37.

38.

39.

40.

41.

42.

43.

44.

45.

WHY SHOULD I DO AND HAVE THESE THINGS IN MY LIFE?

46.
47.
48.
49.
50.

Way to go my friend!

tell you something for nothing, the hard work that you have done here represents a lot for the type of person that you are and that you strive to become.

It is said that (and we should go into this in more detail further on) if the WHY is large enough, then the HOW will appear. Above, you have just completed some amazing reasons as to why you want to improve your life

4. A MATTER OF CHOICE

"THE CHOICES WE MAKE TODAY DEFINE THE QUALITY OF OUR LIFE TOMORROW"

DIGGING DEEP

DARING TO DREAM

A MATTER OF CHOICE

CREATION

Once you have completed your list of your top 100 dreams (or more), we do not stop dreaming, so every time something comes into your mind, add it on to the end of the list as you can constantly revisit this, check things off, add things and so on.

As you can see, there are many things that you would like out of your life – some large, some small and some may even appear a little strange – we now need to focus on what is most important to you. After all, if you were to spread your energy and efforts too thinly, it would be probable that you do not achieve these dreams because as we said near the start this does take time and effort on your part and the aim here is to refine that focus so that it is like a laser beam probing into your future.

However, more than this, we live in a very competitive world and some dreams (to some extent) may involve a certain level of commitment and focus – there may only be one position for that promotion, or there may only be one gold medal to win in your event – this all is down to personal choice and values.

What you would like to do in the future?

These can be things that you would love to do with your career, sports that you would like to have a go at, activities that you would like to do to help other people or qualifications that you would like to get for yourself.

And this means that if you want to achieve big dreams, you do require a great amount of focus and dedication. The bigger the dream, the more focus and dedication is required.

So going on from here, you will refine the things you want to do, step by step, so that you can identify the very best ones to start out with.

Once you have done this, in the next exercise, you can start converting them into powerful, riveting goals through a life changing goal setting process. Ones that will drive you forward towards their actualization.

4.1 REFINING YOUR LIST

From the work that you have done above, we now have a significant list to work towards. You have clearly identified a number of things (100 in fact, for the time being) that you want to create for yourself. Sometimes looking at it now can be a little overwhelming, yet at the same time, pretty exciting.

We are now going to spend some time going through this list in order to refine it a little bit and to do this, we will use the following steps and go through them in more details on the next few pages: -

"Box It Up"

Put into storage for the time being those dreams that are not quite right for now.

"Prioritise"

Identify your top dreams for each area of your life.

"Finalise"

Cut these down to an appropriate list to start working towards straight away.

4.1.1 "Box It Up"

This first step is really simple – go back through your list of 100 dreams and rate them in order of importance and priority to you – if one is high up on your list, rate it with an "A", if it is not that important, mark it "B" and those with a lower priority, draw a box around them.

This will show that they are less important to you right now and are ones that you do not really need to or want to focus on in the immediate future. We found that in doing this exercise and going back through them, some of them could easily be attained right now, just because they had been brought to our attention and this can be exactly the same for you.

It will be obvious which dreams should be added to your "box" list when you compare them to those ranked "A" and "B" – they make lack passion or substance and may also seem somewhat insignificant when compared to those higher up your rankings.

You may also notice that they could have little connection to those things that fill you with a sense of pride or meaning or those that make you happy and fulfilled. They may also conflict slightly with you current values and needs in life that you identified earlier on.

One final thing to look at when doing this. How many of these dreams could you combine together? Are there things that could be done at the same time yet you previously saw them as completely separate items on your "to do" list?

An example of this could be – you want to learn to scuba dive and you also want to travel. Maybe there is somewhere that you could visit, and do the lessons there at the same time?

Or maybe you could write your book based on all the different experiences that you decide to go on from now on – visiting new places or eating new foods and writing about them?

The important thing is to "box" as many dreams as you can for the time being.

Something very important to remember is this – **just because you are boxing them does not mean that you are forgetting about them** – they are obviously important to you for a reason. And just like putting something in storage, we are always able to go back and get it out when we are finished with those things we would like to attend to right now.

4.1.2 "PRIORITISE"

Before we start going through those that are most important to you, or highly ranked, it is worth making sure that you are having some sort of balance in all areas of your life.

Sometimes, people only focus on goals and dreams in one or 2 areas – these typically being careers and health but rarely elsewhere. This can leave a person being an extremely high achiever in these areas and yet stunted, confused and unhappy elsewhere.

Most of us have read stories about hugely successful business owners having heart attacks or unhappy families behind the scenes, or the stay-at-home mom who yearns for a successful business. This is why, earlier on, we suggested that you explored dreams in all areas of your life, and we will go in to them in a little more detail in the following section.

If you do feel that an area of your own life is not covered that is important to you, feel free to add it in now and on the same note, if any of the above areas do not interest you, and then strike them out.

For each of these areas, in the tables provided below, identify the top 5 dreams that matter most to you in each category.

To do this, take your ranked list and extract those that you are most passionate about, the ones that you would really like to achieve for yourself.

Do not worry if you are unable to cut this down to 5 for now because in a short while, you will find a great technique that will help you to do this.

At the bottom of each of each table, you will notice that there is a section called "Any Distinctions that I Have Made." In this, you can record any patterns that you may have noticed in working on this area of your life. Examples of this may be that you see you are not spending enough time with your family or taking time out for yourself. Or maybe you have realised that the work you currently do is more important to you than you thought it was. Just record them down as they have now been brought to the front of your mind for a reason and as you go on, you will be able to get further clarity on these.

AREA OF LIFE	DREAMS AND ASPIRATIONS
Personal Growth and Excellence	1. 2. 3. 4. 5.

ANY DISTINCTIONS I HAVE MADE: -

AREA OF LIFE	DREAMS AND ASPIRATIONS
Fun and Recreation	1.

2.

3.

4.

5. |

ANY DISTINCTIONS I HAVE MADE: -

AREA OF LIFE	DREAMS AND ASPIRATIONS
Friends and Family	1.
	2.
	3.
	4.
	5.

ANY DISTINCTIONS I HAVE MADE: -

AREA OF LIFE	DREAMS AND ASPIRATIONS
Life Direction	1. 2. 3. 4. 5.

ANY DISTINCTIONS I HAVE MADE: -

AREA OF LIFE	DREAMS AND ASPIRATIONS
Career	1.
	2.
	3.
	4.
	5.

ANY DISTINCTIONS I HAVE MADE: -

AREA OF LIFE	DREAMS AND ASPIRATIONS
Relationships	1.
	2.
	3.
	4.
	5.

ANY DISTINCTIONS I HAVE MADE: -

AREA OF LIFE	DREAMS AND ASPIRATIONS
Contribution	1. 2. 3. 4. 5.

ANY DISTINCTIONS I HAVE MADE: -

AREA OF LIFE	DREAMS AND ASPIRATIONS
Health and Fitness	1.
	2.
	3.
	4.
	5.

ANY DISTINCTIONS I HAVE MADE: -

AREA OF LIFE	DREAMS AND ASPIRATIONS
Finances	1. 2. 3. 4. 5.

ANY DISTINCTIONS I HAVE MADE: -

AREA OF LIFE	DREAMS AND ASPIRATIONS
Spiritual	1.
	2.
	3.
	4.
	5.

ANY DISTINCTIONS I HAVE MADE: -

4.1.3 "FINALISE"

From your original list of 100 dreams and aspirations for your life, you now have a shorter list based on the different areas of your life that you find attractive and important, and that inspire you to take action.

Some may be quite large, maybe to run your own company and others may be relatively smaller, such as taking a trip to somewhere you have not been before or buying yourself a new watch. The number of dreams you end up with here really depends on the size of the dream, how much you want to achieve them and how much capacity you have to go out and get them.

Remember the age old saying that goes something like "we often underestimate what we can achieve in a year but over estimate what can be done in a day" and this is something to take into account when doing this. Often, we get caught up in setting goals for ourselves that we tend to spread ourselves too thinly on the ground and end up achieving none.

When we refine our list to those that are more important to us, and once we achieve them, this gives us the "energy" to take on the next and the next and the next.

If you have a dream on your list that is of significant importance to you, then maybe right now there is only room in the next part of your life for that one dream and a few of your smaller ones. If you set out to achieve one large dream, you then take the risk of splitting your effort and not achieving anything of importance to yourself.

Some of your dreams are smaller and more achievable and this would help you to achieve more of them comfortably – only you can decide how many paths you would like to follow. Sometimes (like we mentioned above) we underestimate the time that we have – some people may be busy parents or could have a highly demanding job. If this is the case, scale back on the number of dreams you want to achieve now.

Right now, you may be able to choose an appropriate number and mix of dreams and goals, and if this is the case, then continue on to **Section 3.2** and fill out the list there.

If not, continue on here and we will be on our way in no time.

Remember, scaling down does not mean that we are getting rid of these dreams – we only want to focus on those which are most important to you right now. Focusing on these will give you the inspiration and motivation required to get the wheels in motion, and once you have gone through the process with the larger ones, it is a lot easier to come back and add to your list.

4.1.4 MORE HELP REFINING YOUR LIST

If you are still struggling to choose which of your larger dreams you would like to work towards, you can use a simple technique called **Dream Weighting** to choose between them. This is a great tool to use when you need to choose between options available to you and takes into account many factors.

1. IDENTIFY THE VALUES YOU WANT TO USE IN MAKING YOUR DECISION

Go back to your **"Looking Inside - Summary Sheet"** and in the chart detailed further on, list the top 5 values for your own life. Those that are most important to you now are more than likely very good criteria upon which to base your decision here. When we work in line with the values that we hold close to our hearts, our inspiration to do what we want to do increases significantly.

Insert these Top 5 Values into their corresponding boxes on the Dream Weighting Worksheet.

2. HOW IMPORTANT IS IT?

Now, for each of these values in the box below them on the sheet, score them from **0 (not important)** to **10 (very important)** to show how relevant they are in comparison with the others.

This is now the importance that you are going to apply, and it is OK to give 2 or more criteria the exact same score.

3. SET IT UP

Now take your list of important dreams, or any really because this can be used at any level, and insert them as row labels down the side of the sheet under the heading labelled "Dreams."

4. SCORING

Taking your first dream in Row No. 1, in the grey box, indicate a score of **0 (badly)** to **10 (very well)** as to how this will be in line with the value indicated at the top.

SO as an example, if your value was "honesty" and your dream was "being part of an inspiring team" would this score high or low against this value? We have listed some examples for you to get a better understanding of this as well.

Continue across to your next value until you have gone the whole way across the 5 columns, and then return to the next row and repeat the process.

5. ADD SOME WEIGHT

Under "How Important is it," (Item No. 2) we made a note of your value score and recorded it in our Dream Weighting chart, so we are now going to weigh each dream.

Multiply your score from the last exercise (item 4 –the figure you listed in your grey box) with the figure shown in the box for "Importance" and write down this in the blank space provided. This column where you record this figure is labelled "Score x Imp."

Again, continue across each column and row until you have weighed each item.

6. TOTAL IT UP

After you have calculated each of the above scores, we need to add up the total weight of each dream that has been compared to your Top 5 Values (each of the figures indicated in the "Score x Imp" boxes.)

Add each of these up and put the final total score (or weight) for each dream in the "Totals" column. This will allow you to compare how well one dream does against the other. The higher the score that you achieve, the better the fit that it has with where you are in your life right now.

DREAM WEIGHTING WORKSHEET

VALUES	Honesty		Fun		Freedom		Love		Wealth		TOTALS
IMPORTANCE	10		4		8		7		5		
DREAMS	SCORING	SCORE x IMP	SCORING	SCORE x IMP	SCORING	SCORE x IMP	SCORING	SCORE x IMP	SCORING	SCORE x IMP	
Travel around the world	8	80	10	40	10	80	5	35	1	5	240
Set a world record in an event	7	70	5	20	5	40	4	28	4	20	178
Achieve a high level of fitness	10	100	4	16	3	24	5	35	4	20	195

So as you can see from this example, based on the dream with the higher score, it could be more important to start working towards that rather than the others on at this present time based on these values and scores

On the following page, we have included a blank copy for you to work on yourself.

DREAM WEIGHTING WORKSHEET

VALUES	IMPORTANCE

DREAMS	SCORING	SCORE x IMP	SCORING	SCORE x IMP	SCORING	SCORE x IMP	SCORING	SCORE x IMP	SCORING	SCORE x IMP	TOTALS

7. REALITY CHECK!

Before you continue on, test each answer with your gut instinct, something that we do not do very often. Our intuition is something that some people have learnt not to listen to and taking some time out to just "feel" what you want to do with your life pays great dividends.

If it feels like the right answer for you, then you know you have selected the most important ones to work on now. If something does not feel quite right, check your scoring and take another look at your dream. Is it in line with the life you intend to make for yourself?

Although it seems like a time consuming and laborious process, this scoring helps us to fully identify the dreams and things we want to do that are most important to us.

It is vital that you are completely comfortable with your choice before you continue. Setting out to achieve something that goes against what we hold close can deter us a great deal. And if you are still not entirely happy, go back through the exercises we have completed so far to see if there is something important that you may have missed out.

4.2 COMPILING YOUR FINAL LIST

Once you have completed the last exercise and have come up with your list of dreams and aspirations that you would like to begin work on immediately, think about how this fits in with some of your other dreams and with the shape of your life. As we mentioned earlier, some of the items can be combined. Take one last look and see if you can combine some of your smaller dreams within these larger ones that you have now identified as being important.

So often, we focus on only one thing and do not realise what else we want to do. When we take a look at combining things, this sometimes has an amazing effect on the results we achieve – for example, someone may have a dream of learning a new skill as well as wanting to meet new people – how about combining the 2 and looking for a group that teaches or does the skill you want to learn and join them.

If you have chosen some really significant dreams to work on, there may only be room for a few smaller dreams to add variety and enjoyment to your life, as remember, we want to work on all areas of life and not just focus solely on one.

Choose a final list of those dreams and aspirations that you can work towards with a sense in inspiration and excitement and a strong likelihood of achieving them. Write these down in the table below, and remember, you do not need to fill in each and every row on this table. In fact, and again please do not quote us here, but research has shown that people who focus on between 3 and 5 dreams at a time have a significantly higher level of success than those who focus on a list of 10. So based on your scoring, list the ones that are high up on the list and the ones that resonate with what you want to do with your life.

MY TOP DREAMS AND ASPIRATIONS

4.3 CHECK IT!

In choosing those that you are going to work towards now, the last thing we need to do is to make sure that they are going to be as good as you imagine them to be. After all, so many things in life appear to be exciting and inviting when we take a first look at them yet they can turn out to be much less attractive when you have achieved them and this is based on our experiences in working towards our life dreams thus far.

Also, this is the reason why people used to tell us "be careful what you wish for in life."

It's a simple check really: On your **Looking Inside – Summary Sheet** you have a list – compare this list to those dreams and aspirations that you have chosen to start off on.

Make sure that they fulfil these things in your life, and if they do not, are these dreams that you should be chasing, or should you perhaps take a look at others. It is much better to remove something from your list now (with only minimal time investment) rather than working for a long period to achieve it only to find out that you are not truly enjoying the rewards of your hard work.

And again, ensure that you are not doing too much – there are only 24 hours in a day and you need to continue doing some things at the same time as pursuing your dreams.

Now that you have taken one last look over them all and are sure that this is the way you want to explore your own galaxy, let's move on to creating powerful, compelling goals and dreams that we guarantee (if you follow our suggestions and guidelines) you will achieve.

5. CREATION

DIGGING DEEP

DARING TO DREAM

A MATTER OF CHOICE

CREATION

As we said at the beginning, most people spend more time on their Christmas shopping lists than they do spending time on creating strategies for an amazing life, and for getting this far, we congratulate you.

Some research done a while back, and don't quote us on these statistics, say that fewer than 5% of the population actually set written goals, and less than 1% of those that do actually achieve them – and that is a fact that is pretty clear and obvious when you take a look at the hugely successful people who have made significant differences in their lives.

Why is it that there is only one Michael Phelps or Tiger Woods when there are many excellent swimmers and golfers out there?

Why is it that Richard Branson and Bill Gates are so hugely successful in what they do?

What is the difference between what they do and what we do?

Yes, we only hear of them now, but the point is, they all started somewhere with the exact same resources that you and I have access to but what was the difference that made the difference in their lives?

The answer is that these goals need to be somehow turned into something compelling for you, something that you want to work towards, and then to organise yourself so that working towards these dreams is a central part of the way that you work day to day.

Being organized about this process is vital, and if you are not organized and do not have some sort of system, then your dreams will stay just that – dreams. By looking at yourself and organizing yourself and working step-by-step in a direction you want to go – that is how it is done.

In this section, we will take a look at ways that you can turn these dreams into reality and create a compelling and inspiring way forward.

5.1 WHY DO IT?

- *Why do we set goals and not achieve them?*
- **How can we ensure that when we set a goal, we got out there and claim them as ours?**
- *What steps are present in the processes of people who have made significant differences in their lives through the use of goal setting?*

We will be the first to admit that in the past we have set out to achieve something, only to find that we started off with a bang and ended up nowhere, wondering why we had not claimed what we started out to get. We have sat back and looked at them thinking "I have followed all the rules, be whatever they were, yet something just did not seem to work."

As you well know, goal setting is a process of setting goals and following a plan of action for the way forward and is used by many people around the world. By setting goals well, we map out our progress along the route to our dreams and keep focused on our ultimate destination. The steps and process that we are about to share with you in the next few pages have totally transformed our lives.

And why are we sharing this with you? For the simple reason that the steps we have come up with will give you a fail-safe way to achieve success in your life. We have put them through some rigorous testing, and with commitment, dedication and imagination, you can do the same in your own life.

We will be honest and upfront with you from the start, because 100% honesty is required the whole way through – this may seem laborious and tiresome and you may want to look for shortcuts and save time, and believe me, in the past we tried to use those shortcuts and paid the price.

This process is hard work, there are no easy ways about it, and for some people, it may not be the right approach and to those people, we wish them every success in their journey. There will also be people who are sitting there saying "Yeah well, I know this stuff already" and to them the challenge we put forward is: So when will you put what you say you know into action?

But as we said, we have put these tools into practice and they work if you work them. They produce results, and we look forward to continually using them each and every day of our lives.

.2 REFRAME YOUR GOALS AND DREAMS

A popular musical has an age-old quote that goes along the lines of "a life lived in fear is a life half lived" and this is so true. What we are going to do now is take those dreams and aspirations from your list and look at them in a different light as something else rather than goals.

First of all, if you look at a game of football, and we are sure you can agree with us that, like it or not, this is possibly one of the most popular games in the world. In order to "win the game" one side has to score more goals than the other. They have approximately 90 minutes in which to do this, and they do so by following a ball around and field and kicking it into a net guarded by a member of the opposite team – commonly known as scoring a goal. During an average match (and we have NO idea what the statistics are here) we would hazard a guess that each team takes (let's say) 10 to 15 attempts at scoring a goal.

Sometimes, no goals are scored and at other times, one team will score many and the other none.

But what we are getting at is this. Not every goal they went for got into the net. And that is the same as the belief that we hold. Why set "goals" for ourself? Why not do something that gets you to put the ball in the back of the net every single time?

Based on observations that have been made of the people we mentioned earlier, we have found that the term "goal setting" has been loosely thrown around so many times. What is the difference that makes the difference in these people lives we kept asking, and in doing so, we found one fundamental point that changes everything in the way you look at your goal.

A promise is something that is described as a declaration that one will give or do something, an assurance, guarantee, oath or pledge giving one's word to do something.

So we began looking back at those goals we had set that we did not achieve and noticed a subtle difference. Despite being committed to them, we were not totally focused on them and therefore did not achieve them.

When reframing our goals as promises that we made to ourselves, we found our inspiration to achieve them changed significantly.

So take a look back at your list.

Can you turn these dreams and aspirations into promises to yourself – promises that you are committed to keeping and following through on?

If you are unable to totally commit to these dreams and turn them into promises that you will keep, then take a look back at the values and needs important to you and see how you can line up your goal so that it is a promise.

One more thing to take a look at is the other exhaustive lists that you made. The reasons why you should have these things in your life as well as what would happen if you don't do them. Remind yourself why you have pushed through this book so far and think about the changes that you really want to make in your life. Surely you can make yourself that promise?

Once you have made up your mind to give yourself nothing less than the best for what you want out of life, complete the following declaration as a commitment to yourself and the next step forward. And if you have the courage, show it to someone close to you as a testament of your commitment.

I, _____

hereby declare that I have reviewed

My Top Dreams and Aspirations

detailed in my list and

as a sign of my commitment and promise

to achieving them,

I hereby sign below to show my integrity, honesty

and courage in taking the next step in my personal

journey.

Signed_____

Name_____

Date _____

As you have now completed and signed your declaration, from this point on we are no longer going to refer to goals, dreams and aspirations – they are now referred to as promises, so congratulations on this step.

Now, take a few minutes to re-write your Top 5 dreams as promises in the table provided below: -

MY DREAM AND ASPIRATION :
MY PROMISE :

MY DREAM AND ASPIRATION :

MY PROMISE :

MY DREAM AND ASPIRATION :

MY PROMISE :

MY DREAM AND ASPIRATION :

MY PROMISE :

MY DREAM AND ASPIRATION :

MY PROMISE :

You have now taken the next huge step towards a compelling future, one that many of the successful people around the world have taken and gained huge rewards in doing so.

Celebrate the fact that you have reframed the way you look at your goals and dreams, knowing that in the future, things will not be the same again – promises are made to be kept and you are well on your way now.

5.3 SETTING PROMISES THE "INSIDE OUT" WAY

We may all have heard of "S.M.A.R.T" goals and other goal setting techniques, and we believe and know that they work for some people, and for others, maybe not.

Whilst they all contain very necessary steps, we felt that some were possibly missing. We do not doubt in any way the what we are going to tell you is not new – we have read these things in many books but in our experience, we have not seen them all combined in one place before, and this is what we intend to do now.

This technique or tool involves **9 vital steps** to put the final touches into your promises. Once you have done this a few times, it will be much easier to do with any you set in the future.

For you to be successful, each promise you set (or dream you work towards) needs to contain the following elements that once worked through, will give you a guaranteed plan of action and way forward to achieving whatever you put your mind to.

I - INSPIRATION

N - NEEDS

S - STRETCH

I - IDENTIFY

D - DECIDE

E - ECOLOGICAL

O - ORGANISE

U - UNBRIDLED

ENTHUSIASM

T - TIME TO CELEBRATE

And these are the 9 steps required to initially formulate your promise and put it into words. You will more than likely realise that you have done many of these things at one point or another, but when combining them in one go, they will produce and create a definite promise and action plan towards what you want to achieve.

So let's get started! Choose your top dream (that is now a promise) and we are going to work on that one step by step.

There will be some places where you need to think about things and write them down – doing this gets it all out in the open and will identify any necessary action that you need to take towards limiting decision and beliefs that you may hold, areas in which you may need coaching or mentoring and so on.

Once you get the hang of it, it will be pretty simple for you to do each and every time.

Following each step, we will share with you how we have applied this in our lives and how it has taken shape and come about. This will give you more of an insight into where we have come from and what we have created in our lives as a result of it. They are deeply personal stories from both of us that we felt inspired to share with you in the hope that it gives you a better understanding of each step.

5.3.1 I – INSPIRATION

> "YOU ARE WHAT YOUR DEEP, DRIVING DESIRE IS.
>
> AS YOUR DESIRE IS, SO IS YOUR WILL.
>
> AS YOUR WILL IS, SO IS YOUR DEED.
>
> AS YOUR DEED IS, SO IS YOUR DESTINY."
>
>   - BRIHADARANYAKA UPANISHAD IV4.5

In order to successfully achieve any significant event in our life, we really need to want what we want to do – in other words, there needs to be a deep, driving desire behind the promise we have set.

Take a few minutes to think of why you are making the promises that you have – be brutally honest with yourself and really push hard and question yourself.

There may be a point where you feel like this is going nowhere, but keep asking WHY again and again.

Why? Why must I do this? Why do I need that? What is it that truly inspires me to get out of bed each and every single morning?

ubconsciously, your mind has no option but to answer your question and ive you a reason and the reason why we fell like moving on to the next tep, or the reason we may feel like "bursting" is because our conscious mind is in a battle with the subconscious.

f you keep asking this question, some people have found that the driving lesire or meaning behind the promise is somewhat emotional, for some it nay come as a sense of relief and for others; it is a moment of complete larity.

his is when you know you have found your "why" and when you know you ave been totally honest and got to the bottom of it. It then becomes so nuch easier to get to work on what you have set out to do as you have ound the true meaning.

the "why" is strong enough, then the "how" will definitely follow.

MY PROMISE:

WHAT DOES THIS PROMISE MEAN TO ME IN MY LIFE RIGHT NOW?

WHAT SIGNIFICANCE AND IMPORTANCE DOES IT HOLD?

WHY IS IT IMPORTANT TO ME THAT I ACHIEVE THIS?

WHAT IS MY DRIVING FORCE (OR TRUE MEANING) BEHIND THIS?

CASE STUDY

GARETH

One of the most incredible teachers and mentors I have ever had in my life is a man fondly referred to as "Doc" by his friends. This man was someone who lived his why each and every day of his life and was not afraid to share his philosophy with people he came into contact with and he had a profound impact on my life personally.

I first met Doc many years ago; when my wife and I decided that it would be better if we separated. I had just got out of hospital again, and to be totally honest, did not see any point to this thing called life and was possibly lower than I thought it possible to go. I had lost faith in any form of "God" and in my own mind; I was a complete waste of space, time and effort. I remember when I first moved into his house – I had never met this man before, neither had I met any of his family but a friend of mine also lived there and had arranged for me to come and stay.

I was pretty broken on all levels and I suppose you could look at it like my foundation was on the verge of collapsing after the house had been bombed. My sleeping patterns were very irregular, my health was at an all time low and my self esteem was nonexistent – I just used to sit on the couch, curled up in a little ball, physically shaking and afraid to speak to anyone. Yet somehow, this man saw something that I was yet to see.

Every day, he would greet me and speak to me. He did not say much, but in his eyes, you could feel that he really meant the words. As time went by, and as I opened up a little bit, he began to ask me questions – some that were easy to answer and others that pushed more buttons than I thought I had – all of them starting with one word – "WHY?"

He also gave me a book to read, and told me that he was not a great fan of books but this was one that he was pretty interested in so could I please read it and explain it to him when I was done.

At first, I could not understand why such a wise person would want me to read something and share my views on it with him, but I supposed that I just felt the need to please him so I took on the task. It took me about 6 or 8 weeks to read the book, a few lines at first because that was all I could concentrate on, then a few pages and finally, I got into the book and read it over and over again so that I could share with him what I thought.

And in this process, I found my "why" for living. It started off as a flicker at first then gradually became brighter and brighter until it hit me like a bolt of lightning.

I remember when I sat down with him to talk about the book. There was an area at the house that we called "The Lay By" and it was right next to the swimming pool. Growing up in Africa, you get used to having amazing weather, seeing the most beautiful sunsets and just being outside – and I speak for myself here, but it is something that you take for granted. That evening, as we sat down to talk, the sun was just setting and there was cool breeze in the air – I remember it like it was a few hours ago as I sit here and write. And I began to share. And as I began to talk, I began to cry for the first time in a very, very long time. And then I could not talk.

Only when everything was gone from my life did I realise that it was time I actually had to find something to keep me going. Everything that I had previously lived for, my reasons (or so I thought) for being, were gone, I was completely alone and lost, not knowing what to do. He taught me many things and opened my mind a lot. He taught me to believe in anything and nothing both at the same time. He taught me that everything in my life was created by me, nobody else but me - and trust me, that was a fucking hard pill to swallow. But probably the biggest and most life changing lesson that he ever taught me was to never stop believing in the infinite power that was my inner strength. I realised that I lost my own personal why for living a very long time ago, and because I had lost sight of that, everything I did was for something that I thought was my why. This might sound strange to you at first, and I am sure that you will get it soon, but I learnt that the only why I need to have in my life is my gratitude for having a chance to choose any why that I want to.

And that why was freedom. Freedom to be who I wanted to be, freedom to do what I wanted to do, freedom to live my life as it was meant to be lived, no matter what happened. Because when I finally accepted that why, it made every other seemingly impossible why, possible.

And that is what inspires me and keeps me going today.

The fact that I have the choice to say and do whatever I want, and to deal with the consequences that arise as a result of that. If my why is to change the world, then the fact that I can choose that why makes it touch me deeply. You see, I gave up my own personal power many years ago, due to my own choices, and I guess you could say it led me down a pretty rocky road and in doing so; I took a few people down that road with me. I didn't think that there was a way out of it so I made a few different choices, but Doc showed me that even though it felt like I had nothing left, somewhere deep down inside, something special was still there.

And that night, on the other side of the world, watching the sun set and feeling the cool breeze on my face, my dream came alive again. I knew that it would take a lot of work. In fact, I knew it would take a HUGE amount of work. But the fact that I had been given another chance to find my personal why – when many people don't even begin to realise theirs – was reason enough for me to keep going.

Since that day, yes I have had challenges and difficulties, and at times, I will be the first to admit that sometimes I could actually have just thrown the owel in and said "fuck this shit" but my why keeps me going. Doc taught me something upon which my whole life is now based and that was to just be me no matter what anybody said or did or thought. And that lesson stays with me every single day.

5.3.2 N - NEEDS

Have you ever noticed how you cannot lose weight for another person or get healthy for another person? It is the same with promises that we set – they need to be your own and what you, yourself, specifically need in your own life – not what anyone else needs, or what anyone else wants for you. They have to be things that you want to go out there and achieve.

If it is not for you, then no matter how hard you try, you will not succeed, because your subconscious mind is not focused on it completely because it is not yours.

One very important thing that we need to get our heads around is that we need to stop worrying about everyone else's lives' and start worrying and focusing on ourselves. When starting out, this was a rather foreign topic to us as we felt there was an element of selfishness in doing this. We began to stop comparing ourselves to other people and what they had in their lives when we realised that there was no way we could understand their values and beliefs.

However, what we started to notice and realise was that when we focused on what we needed, everything else naturally started to naturally fall into place as we aligned ourselves with the other steps that followed later on.

When setting out, again, you also have to be completely honest and take a hard look at what you want to do and say "Is this within my own personal capabilities?" or in other words "is this realistic for me?" There will be some things that we are not physically capable of achieving or doing so it is important that you do not set yourself up for disappointment at the outset as this can have a very negative impact on what you do next in your life.

Something that each and every one of us has that is extremely important to us is time. Appreciate the value of time that you have in your own life – this is basically the only chance that you have to do what YOU want to do, nobody else's. You cannot afford to live your life for other people because sooner or later you will realise that you are doing this and will resent it.

It has been said that hell on earth could be defined as meeting the person that YOU could have been if you had done what it was that you wanted to do with your life – is that something that you want ? How do you go about creating the best you, so that if you were to meet yourself, you could hug them and say that I know and love you and am proud of you – it's about YOU! Helping yourself to get what you want out of your life gives you more ways to help other people.

Earlier on, we took a look at your values and. The promises you make need to be in line with these – if they are not, you will find that there is an internal struggle and it can be extremely difficult (although not impossible) to achieve.

Taking all these into account, you will see now why it is important for your promise to be yours and not that of anyone else.

Take a few moments to reflect on the questions that follow.

MY PROMISE:

IS THIS SOMETHING THAT I TRULY NEED OR AM I DOING IT FOR SOMEONE ELSE IN MY LIFE?

IS THIS WITHIN MY OWN PERSONAL CAPABILITIES?

IF I WERE TO ACHIEVE THIS IN MY LIFE, HOW WOULD IT MAKE ME FEEL?

IS THIS IN LINE WITH THE VALUES I HOLD TRUE AND CLOSE TO MY HEART?

IF I DO NOT REALISE THIS PROMISE IN MY LIFE, WHAT WILL THAT MEAN TO ME?

CASE STUDY

GARETH

One of the greatest inspirations I have ever met in my life was a young girl called Keziah. I met her many years ago when I used to volunteer at the church I attended – I used to help out at the Youth Group on a Friday evening and she was one of the regulars who attended. When I first met her, she was still a teenager, but her passion for what she wanted to do with her life touched me deeply.

I loved my time of volunteering because it was something that, for the first time in so many years, I wanted to do. I think at first it was a way of getting back in touch with the young person inside of me who had died many years ago, but as I attended more and more, I slowly started to see that sharing my story with young people, and people in general, could change their lives.

Working with drug addicts can be challenging. Very challenging actually, especially when you are one of them. Most of my life was spent using drugs and drinking more than I should have. Drugs controlled my life and there was a time when it was all that I could think about to get through day despite the fact that I had an amazing family who loved and cared for me deeply.

I got to the stage when, for me, the only way out was to just "get out of everything" and waking up and realising that I had to change something was pretty difficult. At first, I used my children to keep me away from drugs. Having them around gave me a reason to not do drugs. I began attending meetings and started on my road to recovery, and it helped. Yet deep down inside, it was not for me or something I felt I could do and this led me to a few "relapses" as they are referred to. No matter how hard I tried, I just could not seem to do it. After a few months, it got to the day that my children left the country. I remember sitting on the floor in the airport, field with dread because now I had to find some reason to sort my life out as my reason for living was physically gone. I had no idea when I would ever see them again, and this may sound a little drastic but that was how I felt that day.

So I went to a meeting. And I opened my heart to strangers for the first time and spoke of my fears and my challenges. But more than that. I found that when I pushed through the barrier, I started to want to do it for myself. It was frustrating at first, but I kept going. And I kept going. It began to feel good to live without drugs and I began to "feel" again.

And then I met Keziah. Here was a young girl who did what she did because it was what she wanted to do. She was not afraid to speak about, and she was not afraid to share what she wanted out of her life. And she asked me what I wanted to do.

Not just a general question that I could joke about. She looked me in the eyes and asked "what is it that you truly want to do even if it sounds totally crazy" and I guess I got it that day. What it means to be truly selfish and not have selfish be a bad word.

Since that day, I can honestly say that I have had one truly bad relapse that lasted about 6 weeks. It was not fun. In fact, it felt like I had undone 7 years or hard work in a very short period of time. Because I lost sight of what I wanted and what I needed. I had allowed myself to give in to the needs of other people rather than focusing on my own stuff. But years later, a brief message from Keziah via Facebook reminded me of my needs and got me back on track, along with the help of other people.

In 2010, a few months ago actually, Keziah was killed in a car accident.

Over the years since I first met her, she had studied and was working with children, sharing her faith and beliefs. She was doing something that she wanted to do and had spoken about many years ago. She was 21 years old at the time of her death, and was busy planning her wedding.

I will never forget her because her question as a 13 year old to a grown man made me realise how important it was to focus on my needs. After all, if I can't give myself what I need and would like out of life, there is no way that I will truly be able to give to others.

5.3.3 S – STRETCH

Before we start this step, no disrespect is meant using this term – but does your goal make you sit back and draw in a deep breath? Or do you look at it and say to yourself "yeah, that will do for now?"

Does it stretch you and get you out of your current comfort zone, because if it doesn't, you may as well not bother setting out on your journey. Comfort zones are exactly what they claim to be – zones we have in our lives that keep us comfortable because everything is safe and guaranteed.

Your promises need to stretch you and make you grow, they need to get you out there doing new things, learning new things, because let's be honest and face facts here – if you knew everything you needed to know and have been doing everything you needed to do, why have you not achieved these things already?

We always need to grow – no growth = death!

If you are not stepping outside of your comfort zone on a daily basis, you are not moving forwards.

Make your goals stretch you on a continual basis.

DO MY PROMISES STRETCH ME AND MAKE ME GROW OR DO THEY KEEP ME SAFE AND IN THE SAME PLACE?

CASE STUDY

JEROEN

I was driving up north to a small Island called Texel, one of five Islands Holland has. As I lived all the way down South, it was about a 3 hour drive. Rotterdam, Amsterdam, Den Helder and then over the Mansdiep, just a short boot trip to Texel. It was the first time I had ever been to the island; a very cosy, natural place with not too many houses, with a population of just under 14,000, and probably as many sheep.

We got to the Hotel. A nice picturesque place just outside the city centre.

As I was unpacking my bags, it all came back to me; I realised that tomorrow was going to be a big day. Tomorrow was the day that I had decided that I would jump from an aeroplane – my first ever sky dive. And I was terrified. I had done some crazy things in my life, but none as crazy as this, and I began to wonder if I had made the right decision.

The next day after breakfast we drove up to the small airport that was on the island. They call it an airport, but actually it was a landing strip with a building next to it. We went to the building, where we had to read through some paperwork and sign that we would take all responsibility in case it didn't lead to a happy end. After handing in the paperwork, a gentleman told us to hang around for a while and we would be collected to join in on our first day of training.

In the class we had to wear this silly pair of red overalls, which were slightly undersized and uncomfortable. We also had to put on these crazy orange helmets and to make it even worse, we then had to attach an empty sack on our back. During the class, the instructor began explaining everything that could go wrong.

One of the things he told us about was something called a twister; where all your lines get twisted after opening your chute. "Hmmm nice one" I thought silently to myself.

We went through how to hold our bodies, where to look and how to count and then, when our chutes should open automatically as it was a static line jump. This basically means that your parachute is connected via something to the airplane and opens automatically after a few seconds. I actually didn't care how it was attached – I just wanted to get to the ground safely and wondered what I was actually doing here.

The big day arrived the next morning. The weather was good enough for our first jump. We put on the same silly outfits, however, this time without the empty sack. This time we had a real parachute on our back, and I actually did not care about the crazy red overalls and orange helmet. Oh yeah; this time round we also got goggles.

There were 12 of us in the group, silently walking towards a very small plane and when the door (well actually it was more of a shutter) opened, we noticed that there were no chairs.

So all 12 of us were stuffed into the plane along with the pilot and an instructor. We took off and you could feel the excitement rising in that little airplane.

After a few minutes, I looked out of the windows and I could see the whole island below, surrounded by water. A beautiful sight to take in and I wished that I could just sit and look at it for longer.

But then something happened that really made my heart beat even faster than it already was. The shutter opened, and there was a immense noise of engines and wind.

"Wow, that is quite scary, such a big opening in such a small airplane" was all that went through my mind, and on top of that, the instructor pointed at the person sitting next to me; " You first" he said.

The guy moved himself closer to the opening, got two legs out of the airplane and I could see the look on his face. The instructor shouted "1,2,3 go, go, go!" And off he went. Next to go was a girl, same procedure, 1,2,3,go go, go gone.

By this time, I could feel my heartbeat pounding in my throat. "Next. You." I heard and realised that he was pointing at me.

I moved myself to the opening, got my legs out and the force of the wind blew them around from side to side. All I could do right now was hold on tight to the edge of the plane and then I looked down.

All that was racing through my head was "How on earth am I going to land on such a small island, with no experience of flying a parachute and all that water", and all of a sudden, there was no way back - 1,2,3, Go, go, go.

And I jumped, head up looking to at the plane and a hollow back as explained in the training, silently counting in my head and praying that my chute would open OK. I felt the jerk and breathed a sigh of relief – it had opened. But as I look up, I saw something else. That 1 in a 100 chance - all my lines were twisted together.

That's right ! I had a twister!

And all I could do was what I had been told. Hands up, pulling the lines away from each other and make a cycling motion, and luckily I slowly started moving in circles, unwinding my lines, up to a moment that everything came loose and with a little bounce I was free.

I grabbed my steering handles, pulled them towards me and then there wa silence. The most beautiful feeling, flying, gliding through the sky. In full control of where I wanted to move to. Free as a bird. And an amazing view! I never believed that stretching myself to that limit could give me such an amazing feeling, one that I will never forget.

5.3.4 I – IDENTIFY

To borrow a quotation from Alice in Wonderland: -

"WOULD YOU TELL ME, PLEASE, WHICH WAY I OUGHT TO GO FROM HERE?"

"THAT DEPENDS A GOOD DEAL ON WHERE YOU WANT TO GET TO," SAID THE CAT.

"I DON'T CARE WHERE . . ." SAID ALICE.

"THEN IT DOESN'T MATTER WHICH WAY YOU GO," SAID THE CAT.

If you do not know what you want, you can be certain that you won't get anything. When writing out your promise, you need to know exactly what you want so that you can go out there and get it – do not be ambiguous or vague as this allows rationalisation to creep in – state it exactly how you want it and when you want it by – concise, clear and straight to the point !

The more specific and clear you are, the more chance you have of going out there and doing it, because your subconscious mind knows exactly where you would like it to go.

For example, if you have a financial ideal, use specific figures and if you want to reach a certain weight, state it specifically.

In finishing off this point, you will also need to know how and when you have reached your destination – what has to happen in order for you to see the attainment of it?

So before we take some time to re-write our promises in a clear and concise way, quickly ask yourself these questions in relation to what you are working on: -

HAVE I SAID EXACTLY WHAT I WANT?

DO I KNOW WHEN I WANT IT BY?

WHAT WILL I SEE, HEAR AND FEEL WHEN I REALISE MY PROMISE?

SO as an example, we have written one for you to follow, and I am sure that many of you have come across examples that have been structured like this. As we said at the start of this book, we have found many things along the way that have been profoundly useful and we therefore share them openly with you because they have utmost relevance in what we do.

"It is now 26th April 2007, and as I look up and see the brightly coloured parachute open above me, feeling the wind rushing past my face and all around me, I look out over the beautiful countryside knowing that I have successfully jumped out of a moving plane at 30,000 feet and my heart is filled with pride as I know that I have conquered my biggest fear in life."

You have the idea, right? Now re-write your promise to yourself, knowing that this is a step towards realising something you have always dreamt of doing.

MY CLEAR AND CONCISE PROMISE TO MYSELF: -

CASE STUDY

JEROEN

I met her 10 years ago. A very good friend of mine actually met her first, on a holiday in Greece. He one day organised a double date, her and a friend and then the two of us. We got tickets for a huge party called " Inner City" organised by ID&T.

The party was great; the connection was slightly uncomfortable though. It was only in the very last moments of the evening, that we started dancing which subsequently turned into a passionate kiss. On the way back to Arnhem, where both of the girls both lived, and where my friend and I had booked a hotel, our hands met in the car, and it felt good. The whole way back to Arnhem, which was about an hour and a half's drive, we held hands without saying a single word.

We got the girls home safety and made our way back to the hotel. It was about 6 o'clock in the morning and we made it very clear to the receptionist that we did not want to be disturbed until at least 2pm. We got to the room which was nice and warm and my friend and I sat down and reviewed the evening, both agreeing that we had just had a splendid night out.

All I know is that as soon as my head hit the pillow, I was fast asleep instantly and the next thing I heard was an unexpected, irritating ringing noise. It was the phone that woke me up, so naturally, I assumed it was 2pm. I looked at the time and was slightly confused as it said that it was only 11am. I picked up the phone, just a little bit annoyed as this was not what we had agreed with the hotel receptionist.

Instead, I heard a lovely ladies voice on the other side of the line that I instantly recognised and I relaxed straight away. It was her. She had come to the hotel to surprise me, so I invited her to come up to the room, where she jumped onto the bed and we just embraced each other. I don't know how long it was for because time stood still.

From that day we started dating. We went to nice restaurants. We stayed in beautiful hotels, retreats and did so many other romantic things together.

However, there was only one issue. I did not want to commit to a relationship. I blamed my parent's divorce and did not want to go through the same stuff, which I now know is actually impossible. But this amazing lady kept showing, and I started pushing her away; too afraid to open up and give myself to someone else.

I moved to Belgium and we still kept seeing each other. Then I moved to London and even then, we still kept seeing each other. I got really comfortable with her around me and started giving myself more and opening up more, and it even got to the stage that I did not want her to leave. So I asked her to come and live with me, and in her happiness, she cried.

I gave her a hard time for many years, by pushing her away. But her persistence, trust and belief brought us closer together. Close enough that both of us decided to have a child after living together in London for about 2 years. I always thought that when I was ready and decided to have a child, it would just happen.

But things actually worked out a slightly different. We made the decision in 2007, and each and every month there was a bit of disappointment. I remember one day when the monthly cycle was late. This was it we thought. One day passed, then another and then yet another. Could this be it? Again! Another disappointment. And this went on for many months.

We decided to go for an ICSI, something that I was not a great fan of because I think that nature takes care of it and it would happen when it happened. But in a relationship you are not alone and it is not just my opinion that counted.

They took something from her, I donated something from me, this got mixed together and it was time for cell division. That all went ok and an appointment was made to put back 2 of the embryos. This was just before Christmas, so the two of us (and the embryos) went to see my mother and her husband on the other side of the world. She lives in a place called Nouvelle Caledonie, between New Zealand and Australia.

Exciting times for us. We were having a great holiday until our last week there, when we hit a bit of a downer. It hadn't work and none of the embryos had nested.

Of course we did not give up and continued again in the new year. After a few more months of trying we started to think about another round of ICSI treatment. But this time it was not necessary. Mother Nature stepped in and took care of it. It was May 2009 that she fell pregnant and we are now the very happy and proud parents of our son Luca. A wonderful soul who makes me feel warm inside just by thinking about him.

In a few weeks time, we travel again to Nouvelle Caledonie, only this time as proud parents, sharing Christmas with Luca and his grand parents and celebrating the fact that being totally clear about what we wanted out of life would one day be given to us.

5.3.5 D – DECIDE

"USING THE POWER OF DECISION GIVES YOU THE CAPACITY TO GET PAST ANY EXCUSE TO CHANGE ANY AND EVERY PART OF YOUR LIFE IN AN INSTANT."

ANTHONY ROBBINS

Keeping promises involves a certain level of decisiveness – in fact, it requires a pretty big decision on your part, and once you are clear on why you want what you want, have an action plan and combine this "doing" with a true decision, then you are on your way to success in your life. This could probably be the most extensive session in this process, and probably because it is one of the most important ones you could do.

One thing about decisions is that, when made properly, they create commitment. A commitment to doing something totally different than before. This is what a true decision really is.

Think about what your current level of commitment is towards your future. Put it this way, if you went sky diving, how committed would you be to pulling the cord for the parachute to open? You read Jeroen's story earlier on about his experience. Your promises require a very similar level of commitment.

Commitment also involves a certain level of accountability in our lives. Sometimes - in fact - most times it can be seen that when you tell someone you trust what you are setting out to achieve, it increases your level of commitment. Do you make yourself accountable for what you do? Who and what accountability have you given?

You will not be able to give up if you have been honest with the true meaning of your promise as the start of this process. Are you determined to get where you want to be? Not one successful person out there - from Richard Branson and Bill Gates to Michael Phelps and Lance Armstrong - does anything successful without commitment and hard work – in fact, when you do your research, you will notice that most, if not all, of the successful people in the world have had to make sacrifices and changes in their lives in the attainment of their individual promises.

What are you prepared to give up whilst you go out there and change your life? What are you not prepared to sacrifice and why? You have to be willing to pay the price of getting to your destination, as fortunately, or unfortunately for some, everything has a price and this is sometimes the hardest thing for some people to decide. The power of commitment to your promise is huge.

Realising this is a major step towards getting there so take a good hard look at it.

In making a firm commitment, just know that the first time you take action is always the worst time, especially if it something totally new to you – like Marmite, you will either love it or hate it so why not get it out of the way as soon as possible?

Finally, more often than not, people settle for mediocrity in their own lives. They turn around and say "well I did the best that I could so maybe this will do as I am a little better off than before anyway." It is not about doing the best that that you can, if you are truly committed to your promise, it is about doing whatever it takes – this is now playing at an entirely different level and shows true commitment to where you will be.

Be prepared to pay full out, rather than "doing the best you can."

Say to yourself **"I WILL NOT TOLERATE MEDIOCRATY ANY LONGER; I WILL NOT SETTLE FOR LESS, I WILL NOT COMPROMISE ON THE ATTAINMENT OF MY GOALS."** Greatness in life is non-negotiable and we often times have too many negotiable things going on.

What do you need to make non-negotiable in your life?

George Bernard Shaw was quoted as saying something along the lines of **"Doing what needs to be done will not make you happy at first, but it will make you great!"**

This decision and subsequent commitment, combined with the action steps provides you with momentum, and that momentum is what keeps you taking action and staying committed to doing whatever it is that you want to do with your life. Often, once we have made up our minds, committed to a plan of action and started working towards things, providence moves in and things happen very quickly, so be prepared!

MY PROMISE:

ON A LEVEL OF 0 TO 10, HOW COMMITTED AM I TO THIS PROMISE?

HAVE I MADE MYSELF ACCOUNTABLE TO SOMEONE, AND TO WHOM?

IS THERE ANYTHING THAT I NEED TO GIVE UP ON MY WAY TO ACHIEVING THIS?

AM I PREPARED TO GIVE THIS UP?

WHAT THINGS DO I NEED TO MAKE NON-NEGOTIABLE IN MY LIFE?

THIS SERVES TO CONFIRM THAT I AM COMMITTED TO TAKING ACTION

TOWARDS MY FUTURE AND THAT I AM NOT PREPARED TO GIVE UP

ALONG THE WAY TO ACHIEVING MY LIFE'S DESIRES

Signed _____

Date _____

Decisions also involve a certain level of preparation, and we definitely need to get ready for things to be different, but more importantly, to be done differently.

In other words, do you have all the correct ingredients for your recipe? What is it that you need to go to the store and buy before you can start baking your cake or cooking your meal?

There are many times that people set out to do something without taking time to check that they have everything that they need, only to come to a grinding halt, de-motivated and put off, because they did not check that they were good to go.

Do you have everything that you need? Do you need to learn or do something new in order to get to where you want to be?

Remember that this could be as a result of a setback that you may have had in the past in doing what it is that you want to do. Take a few minutes to realise that if we actually knew everything that we needed to know (and I think we said this earlier) we would already be doing everything we aspire to do.

Earlier on, we also asked the question "what is holding me back?" If there were things holding you back, what are they and how will you go about rectifying them?

Do you know of someone that has achieved something similar to what you would like to do? What steps would they take, or did they take, to get where they are today? Picture in your mind someone who has already accomplished one or more of the very large promises that you have made, and this should be a real person.

You see, in pursuit of whatever place we think we want to be, there are many people, dozens... maybe millions of them who have succeeded before us. And all these people that have gone before us hold clues and tips as to how they got there.

One of the main reasons, we believe, why many people do not reach their promises is that they don't have the same core level beliefs as people who've succeeded where you may have given up before. Successful people have very different beliefs from those who have never tried or who have attempted the same thing repeatedly. But this is rarely even considered... What beliefs do you need to change?

Here is a brief exercise you can do to experience the power of belief:

Pick an area of life that isn't working for you at all - health, weight, bad habits, relationships, career, financial, sports, school... you choose. Be honest with yourself and take some time out to think about the answers to these questions, and you can jot them down on a scrap of paper if you like.

Have you planned out everything you need to do to reach your goal?

Are you confident you'll absolutely reach it?

When you make a mistake, do you often get down about it and get stalled?

Do you believe you deserve success, even though there are millions of others who are just as deserving, but give up?

Will factors outside your control dictate whether you are going to succeed or not?

If it would take many months or even years to achieve your promise, is that OK with you?

Is following through on what you know are right decisions in this area somewhat difficult?

There are literally hundreds more questions, but we'll stop there. Now, imagine the MOST successful person you know of in that area of life. And look at the questions again. What do you imagine their answers would be for each of them?

The answers, most definitely, are completely opposite. Can you see now how disempowered, false beliefs hold you back?

You may have answered yes to some of the questions above and in doing what you have done so far, you may have come to realise that there are a few things that you need to work on in order to start creating an even more amazing life than you have now. For some, this may cause a bit of concern, however, the answer is here for you.

Do you have a coach or mentor who will help you through the entire process of getting to where you want to be? Again, more often than not, many people think that they can go it alone, yet if you take a closer look at 99% of the successful people out there – be it business, sport, whatever – they all have one vital person – their coach. Your coach will help you work through things that you feel are limiting you and holding you back; they will help you identify these areas and work together with you on them in order to help you do what you know you want to do.

Do you need to work with someone in some form of strategic partnership? Do you have a team in place that you can work with? Let's say you want to get fit – do you have regular training partners and a fitness instructor or personal coach?

Many people are intent on achieving things on their own so why not try a different approach, and for once work together with people. Share your journey, and subsequent success in creating an amazing life with a team of like-minded people.

After the 2008 Olympic Games, Michael Phelps stated that there was no way he could have achieved his promise (we quoted that) of 8 gold medals if it were not for two things – his coach and his team mates. It's pretty obvious then, isn't it?

One of the most important pieces of advice that we would give you is this right here - when identifying or choosing a coach and team to work with, always make sure that these people are eating out of their own kitchen - in other words, are they an example of what and where you would like to be in the future ?

Be prepared for whatever comes your way along your journey. As you know, your promises are YOURS, they are what you clearly want out of your life, and have taken action and made a massive commitment towards – this can be shown by the simple fact that you have read this far.

We mentioned being sure exactly why you want what you want, what it means to you and what it will mean if you do not achieve it. Along your path, you will discover that some people are willing to do anything to achieve their promises and they may not have come across our book to meaningful success in their lives.

The only advice we can offer is to learn from any experiences you have of people sabotaging your plans in one way or another, and again, this can be dealt with simply by ensuring you have a coach and/or mentor on board with you.

So now that you have thought about everything that you need to get going, take a few moments out to briefly write down your learning, and if action needs to be taken in order to ensure that you have all you need. Then do some research and find out who can provide you with what you need.

MY PROMISE :

DO I HAVE EVERYTHING THAT I NEED?

WHAT NEW SKILLS DO I NEED TO LEARN TO HELP ME?

DO MY BELIEFS LINE UP WITH MY PROMISE FOR MY LIFE?

IF NOT, HOW I AM GOING TO RESOLVE THIS?

DO I HAVE A COACH TO HELP ME ALONG THE WAY?

DO I NEED A MENTOR?

DO I NEED TO CREATE A TEAM OF LIKE-MINDED PROMISE KEEPERS?

AM I PREPARED FOR WHATEVER COMES MY WAY?

CASE STUDY

GARETH

I don't know about you, but sometimes I do some pretty crazy things and I remember sitting down and thinking about something that would really push me on every level possible. The last time I actively ran was when I was about 15 years old and up until then, I was a pretty good runner, both long and short distances. However, other things became more important to me and in my life then, exercise and physical exertion was something that did not really excite me very much. In fact, there was a time when I would rather drive somewhere than walk down to the shop on the corner that is how lazy I got.

So, seeing as I was living in one of the biggest cities in the world, I decided that maybe it was time to run again and as I picked up the paper on the tube, I saw an advert for places for the London Marathon through a charity that was very close to my heart – Action on Addiction. When I got to the office, I sent off an email, and did not think any more of it. After all, the marathon was about 6 weeks away, I had not done any exercise for a number of years and on top of that, and I would also have to raise a significant amount of money for the place so I did not expect anything to come about.

That evening, I got a phone call and I was given a place, on the condition that I raised the money.

So here I was. Just given a place in the London Marathon – 26.2 miles. 42.2 kilometres. £1,750.00 in fund raising. And 6 weeks. 6 frikkin weeks! It was racing through my mind the whole way home and as I walked through the door, the size of the task I had just agreed to hit me in the face like a ton of bricks.

Before I go on, I guess that I should add a little physical fact in to this current situation. At the time, I was 34 years young. I say young, because I don't really believe in age – I think it is just a number and therefore, that is what I just say. Anyway. At the age of 26, I had my first heart attack as a result of drugs, and at 32, I had my second heart attack (no drugs involved this time around fortunately.) In hospital after my second heart attack, the doctor sat down in front of me and gave me a very serious warning that there was a strong possibility that the next one could be the final one for me and that was pretty scary to hear. So the fact that I was now considering taking on one of the most gruelling physical challenges that you could put yourself through could be seen by some as something stupid, and right now I will say that I do not, in any way or form, recommend this to anyone.

And then I sat down with these 9 steps that you are currently going through, and I spent the entire night going through each and every single step with this dream of mine as the sole focus. I made sure that I got everything out on paper and the next day, I started working.

found myself a personal trainer, and believe me, I went through a few of them because when I mentioned my previous health conditions, 99% of them refused to help me out. I finally found a trainer and sat down and told him everything. He explained to me the effects a marathon can have on a physically healthy body, just so that I was fully aware of everything. I even agreed to sign a piece of paper that basically said if I did during this challenge of mine, it was all of my own doing and had nothing to do with him.

But more importantly, overnight I literally had to change everything about the way I approached my life. I had to change my diet, my way of life, my training routine, my way of thinking – just about everything. At first, it was extremely difficult. The weather in England during at that time of the year is not very enjoyable and there were times when it took everything that I had to get out of bed. When I faced challenges, I spoke to my coach and went through things with him and that was what he was there for. He was there to help me and guide me along the way. I began speaking to other people who had run marathon's before to find out how they dealt with "hitting the wall" and what got them through.

regularly had to monitor my progress and push myself past what I believed possible for myself as I only had a very short time to do this, but deep down inside, I knew that when I did this, these 9 Steps would face their most punishing and gruelling test, so I kept going.

The day of the marathon itself is one that will stay with me for the rest of my life. I spoke to my mom and sister the night before, because yes, deep down inside, I was pretty scared. I knew what I was about to put myself through, but at the same time, I had done things completely different to anything I had done before so I had faith that I could achieve this. Through my coaching, I had learnt so many techniques and tips that could help me and through sharing with others, I had ways to get around the hurdles that lay ahead. Now all that was left was for me to put it all into practice and actually run.

I had set myself a time of 5 hours to complete the marathon – I had to be realistic with myself given that I only had 6 weeks to prepare, and being realistic as you know, is one of the steps this book speaks about. I crossed the line in 4 hours 59 minutes and 10 seconds and realised how that decision and commitment changed things for me in more ways than I thought at first.

Deciding was one thing but actually going and doing something about was something else altogether, and that is what made the marathon possible for me.

5.3.6 E – ECOLOGY

To put into our own words something that we have heard mentioned before – when you take into account the needs of those around you rather than only thinking of yourself, the more inspiration you will have to do what it is that you want to do because you know that it will have far greater benefits.

So when working on your promises, always ensure that you take into account and consider the consequences to all that is around you – in other words, take an ecological approach when setting out.

Think of how it affects you first and foremost, then those close to you such as family and friends following by your social circle, community and society, and finally on a higher level, the world as a whole. Is you promise going to hurt or damage anyone or anything and what impact is it going to have?

In spiritual terms, this can and is often referred to as "Karma" – we sow what we reap in life. Live your life so that every deed and action that you do is returned to you in a way that benefits you rather than holds you back.

In setting out on my promise, have I taken into account the needs of all those around me?

CASE STUDY

JEROEN

So yes, here we were, on our way to Brighton with two lovely friends, G and myself. One of our friends had been so kind as to be our chauffeur, but both of them to had come along to support us.

There was a lot of laughter and jokes in the car, but at the same time, also many moments of silence followed again by even more laughter. One minute the windows closed but then it got too hot. Windows open for a bit and all of a sudden, too cold. Windows closed again, and so the journey continued. You can imagine the vibe that was going on, it was our 1st professional speaking gig and on top of that, it was also for the YES Group in Brighton – something that was very close to our hearts.

After a very interesting journey through the beautiful English countryside, we eventually got to the hotel. And yes, right on the sea front. We parked the car in the hotel car park and took the opportunity to breathe in some cool, fresh sea breeze and just to enjoy the wonderful scenery. Blue sky and the sun reflecting in the water; the perfect place for quiet meditation and peaceful thoughts right before such an exciting event.

Now it was time for some action! Time to meet with the organiser of the event. We made our way to the second floor of the hotel where we met two people from the Yes Group.

"Aha you must be Gareth and Jeroen from Ego Invenio!"

They were expecting us. It felt so good. It was all becoming so real now. We already started to see the impact and effect that making the decision of following our passion and stepping up had started to have. Now we were on the other side of the events we worked in, looking through new eyes. There were people looking after us, instead of us looking after people. They checked in with us and asked if everything was to our liking and on top of that, there were people on their way to come and listen to us. What a great feeling. The rewards of deciding and stepping up!

The talk went pretty smoothly, but more important than that; we shared from our hearts what we believed to be true and what our message was about. The participants got great value and gave us some very positive feedback, which was for us the icing on the cake given that this was the first time we had stood up in front of a live audience.

When you follow your heart and be true to yourself and others, you just have to take action, knowing that what you say is going to make a difference, no matter how small or large – that is inconsequential in the grand scheme of things. And when you take this type of action, it is amazing how everything falls perfectly into place and new doors open.

 People and opportunities show up. You feel more vibrant, more alive and more excited than you could have though possible. And yes believe it or not, all that just from making the decision that does not just involve you. You take into account everything around you, because it matters to you now.

It does not mean that you won't have any more challenges, or how some people like to call them "problems" in your life. It only gives you better quality problems to face and overcome.

I am so grateful for all the opportunities that we have in life and cannot wait to start inspiring people on a larger scale, to live a healthier and more fulfilling life. It's about time that everyone starts to recognise how great they really are and how much they are capable of. How beautiful it is to add value to other people's lives.

Before I was afraid to step up and speak up. I couldn't speak to a group of people larger than 5 without my legs shaking my voice trembling. I didn't even believe that I would ever be able to conquer that fear.

A few weeks ago, I stood up and spoke in front of a group of 600 people and of course there were nerves, but at the same time, I was quite relaxed about it. I used to say and believe that I was shy because a large part of me only took into account what was going on for me at the time. Now I believe it is just a cheap excuse for not having the guts to grow and share with everyone else what I know to be true.

5.3.7 O – ORGANISE

This is a pretty obvious one, and one that we are well aware of. In order to realize your promise, you need to do more than state it – you need to go out there and DO it. You need to get active, get things going and take the action that is required. Your promises need to be action based and follow some sort of organised plan, they need to make you want to take the steps required, and physically take the steps required towards them.

Picture this as an example, and this is a pretty exaggerated one but you will get the picture. Imagine yourself winning £32,235,700.00 in the lottery; really focus on it with all your might, just being totally in line with it. – see yourself jumping up and down with excitement, seeing the things you will be buying soon and just all the feelings that go with it.

Now!

Back to reality. If you do not 1) find the money for the ticket, 2) choose the numbers and 3) go out and physically buy the ticket, there is no way you will ever win that lottery. So, as we said, this is a pretty exaggerated example, but if you do have an action plan, and physically do what is required, you won't get anywhere.

Some people may call this motivation – personally, we feel that whilst motivation is a very nice feeling and "thing" to have, we have a slightly different approach to this, and again, it has altered our results significantly.

Motivation is not something that we wake up with.

What creates the motivation is the action that we take to moving forward. When we decide to do something, in the moment we can get excited and we can mistake that for what we believe most people may call motivation, but if you notice, that feeling does not last too long.

It is only when you begin taking action towards those decisions that we get momentum, and that is the true motivation we believe.

So now, take some time to list your first few action steps, and always remember that you can come back and add more – this is just to give you the basis and get you going.

MY PROMISE :

WHAT ARE THE TOP 5 ACTION STEPS THAT I NEED TO TAKE IN ORDER TO GET WHERE I WANT TO GO?

1.

2.

3.

4.

5.

OF THESE ACTION STEPS, THIS IS THE FIRST STEP THAT I AM GOING TO TAKE WITHIN 12 HOURS FROM NOW: -

If you struggled with writing down some of the steps, or were not sure what to write, then complete the following: -

WHAT IS STOPPING ME FROM TAKING ACTION?

Beliefs, decisions about the future or what we want to do and more importantly, fear are very real to each and every one of us and are often a big stumbling block, stopping us from even getting our feet off the ground. Identifying them at this stage helps us to work on them, and this will be covered in a later stage of the process – the important thing to do is to write them down here.

Often times, when we take action, the steps we come up with do not take us where we may have expected them to take us, and this sometimes causes people to give up. So what if you have setbacks or minor diversions – these show that you are, in fact, taking action, so celebrate them. Enjoy that you have had the opportunity to learn how not to do it, and take time out to see what you need to either do differently or what it is that you need to learn to do.

AM I PREPARED TO BE FLEXIBLE IN MY APPROACH OR ARE THE ACTION STEPS I HAVE WRITTEN DOWN RIGID AND THE ONLY WAY TO ACHIEVE MY PROMISE?

There may be times when we are following our action plans, when all of a sudden we seem to come to a grinding halt and do not know what to do next. This could be that we have missed out an action step that is required along the way. Pull over, stop and get some clarity on what to do next – come back to this section and work your way through again.

AM I COMFORTABLE WITH THE STEPS I HAVE LAID OUT SO FAR AND AM I PREPARED TO COME BACK AND TAKE A LOOK IF I GET STUCK ALONG THE WAY?

A final suggestion here and another one that makes a huge difference – NEVER, EVER TRY – just DO! Put your action steps into action, don't try and do them, as this basically means inaction or just making an effort and not really achieving anything substantial. If we were to tell you to close your eyes and then try and open them, how would it turn out? If you were to open them, you took the action needed, there was no element of trying, you just did it! When you try and do something, you don't actually achieve it, because there is always a way of doing it.

AM I PREPARED TO DO AND NO LONGER TRY?

CASE STUDY

JEROEN

I was a very mechanical person, like my planning and having and putting systems into place. And even when there is a system in place, to me there is always room for improvement – a way of polishing it up or making it even more efficient.

A very effective way of getting things done in life is to plan your time efficiently.

Although, for most of my life I just went with the flow. I did whatever came across my path and just went with it. I realised that time went by and actually not a lot got done. Until I started reading specific books and going to seminars where the main focus was on success and achieving your dreams. It was there that I saw what all these successful people had in common. They knew how to spend their time wisely.

"IF YOU CAN'T MANAGE YOUR TIME, YOU WON'T BE ABLE TO MANAGE ANYTHING!"

The most common excuses people have are I don't have the money and I don't have the time.

Yet these successful people that got something done, the won money and they lost money and the only thing they had the same amount of was TIME

168 hours per week to be exact.

So, I began to divide my tasks over the amount of hours I had each day and started filling up the week like that. I programmed my iCal (Macbook Calender) with different colours for different categories (work, home, exercise, family, etc) including alarms and all. It worked pretty well to be honest and I noticed that I actually got a lot more done. It also gave me peace of mind, not having to think about all the "stuff" that I needed to do. They just popped up on my phone when I needed to start doing them.

As beautiful as it might sound, it actually did start to annoy me after a while. Because you are not always in the position to do exactly what your alarm is instructing you what to do. And when you don't take care of the task showing on your screen, the next one soon pops up soon and the next one and the next one – you get the picture right? Until you lose the plot and get frustrated.

Systems are brilliant, but you need to leave some space to breath. I started to feel like a robot, living on instructions by the hour.

I had the privilege recently to work with Benjamin J Harvey, a trainer that taught us some amazing tools - including an amazing time management tool. But this time with space for living and having a life too. Based on your 3 personal strengths, you work on your 3 major rocks (the things that when done, your life and business will move forward strongly.) Next to that you still have your daily tasks, but your main focus is always those rocks.

Another major thing that I like about his system is that you keep track of all your achievements on a form and instead of crossing out what you have completed. You highlight them, instead of having a scribbled mess and only noticing all the things that you have not done. You now clearly see what it is that you have achieved during your day.

There is of course more to organising your life than just planning your time and using it more efficiently, but I can tell you that when you master this skill, the rest is going to be peanuts!

5.3.8 U – UNBRIDLED ENTHUSIASM

Have you ever watched a little child the night before Christmas?

They can't sit still, they know that something is going to happen; they have a picture in their mind that they are going to get presents – sometimes they have even written their letters to Santa, explaining exactly what they want. In order to get these presents, they know that they need to go to bed and get to sleep, yet the excitement keeps them awake. Eventually, exhausted, they finally fall asleep, and early in the morning, they are straight out of bed, downstairs and ready to open those presents.

To us, this is how we should feel every morning we wake up because we have another chance to achieve success in our lives. When we have something inspiring to work towards, it is not work, it is passion and excitement and it goes a very long way.

This may sound slightly over the top and exaggerated, but that is the level of commitment and enthusiasm we need to push ourselves towards if we are to do what we want to do. Following each of the steps up until now will awaken that excitement deep within you and will give you the enthusiasm that you need.

MY PROMISE :

DOES MY PROMISE MAKE ME EXCITED AND WANT TO GET OUT OF BED IN THE MORNING AND TAKE ACTION TOWARDS IT?

DOES THINKING OF HOW I WILL FEEL WHEN I ACHIEVE MY PROMISE MAKE ME WANT TO TAKE EVEN FURTHER ACTION?

IF THE ANSWER TO EITHER OF THESE IS "NO" AM I 100% CERTAIN THAT MY MEANING IS TRUE TO ME?

WHAT WILL IT TAKE TO GET THAT UNBRIDLED ENTHUSIASM THAT I NEED?

Another way to look at this - **GET OPTMISTIC!**

People have done things (or similar things) that you want to go out there and do - these promises are therefore attainable, are they not? They have seen their vision, committed and persisted and have reaped the rewards. Be grateful for the opportunity that you have been given to have the open-mindedness to better your life.

Gratitude is the mother of belief, belief is the mother of faith, faith is the mother of optimism and optimism is the mother of persistence. It is said that the secret of our future is hidden in our daily routines, and this is a fact that is very true. One of the easiest ways to uncover the habits that you don't know you really have that create your future (think about that for a while) is by focusing on the things that you are truly grateful for.

When you do this, it uncovers things that you are doing that create the results your currently have in your life. Once you notice these patterns, it then gives you the opportunity to either break them (if they are holding you back) or put more focus on them (when they are driving you forward.)

But more importantly, when look at the line that we mentioned, your belief and faith in the tasks that you undertake is dramatically increased, thereby increasing your optimism and the way that you approach the things you do. In turn, this provides you with the persistence to keep going and this results in new habits which therefore influence the future that you create for yourself. This may sound like a bit of a mouthful when you first read it, but once you grasp and understand this simple principle, radical changes take place.

Starting from today, create a list of 10 things that you are grateful right now – no matter how big or small they may seem. Some people have actually never sat down and written out a gratitude list. Spend a few minutes just reflecting on everything on your list and really connecting with each item as it resonates within you.

At the end of every day, spend a few moments going over the day gone by in your head, the steps that you have taken, the results you have achieved and even the things that you have learnt and add 2 more items, every day, to your list.

Before you go to sleep, pick one of these new items and just have it at the front of your mind as you nod off. Without going into too much detail, this subconsciously prepares your mind for the following day, as rather than focusing on negative things; it has something that you are in touch with to focus on. It also helps you to realise how much you have actually achieved and during the day, when you encounter challenges, it gives you a "boost" to deal with them.

Then, in the morning before you leave home, again for a few minutes, just spend some time looking through your list. Doing this truly creates the momentum and persistence required to continually take positive action towards your personal vision. Now that is something to get excited about, ain't it?

WHAT ARE 10 THINGS IN MY LIFE THAT I CAN BE GRATEFUL FOR RIGHT NOW?

1.

2.

3.

4.

5.

6.

7.

8.

9.

10.

CASE STUDY

GARETH

Sometimes, taking on a huge personal challenge can actually be quite a big thing, especially when it involves radically changing and transforming your own life. Stepping out into the unknown is a daunting task for many people, and I know that in the past, just the slightest change would really unsettle me.

Just over 4 years ago, I made a huge decision to re-locate and start over again. I had been working hard on other areas of my life and felt that it was time to take a step of faith and begin the final piece of my own personal journey, and that was moving countries. Having grown up in Africa my whole life, the thought of living in one of the biggest cities in the world was something that I actually could not really comprehend and if I am honest, it filled me with just a little bit of fear. I did not know anyone who lived in London and had no idea what it really involved – I would need somewhere to live, I would need a job – so many things filled my mind.

But one thing that I had learnt, and started to apply, was that the feeling of fear and the feeling of excitement are so closely linked that we confuse them. And because of that little voice in our head, we often give way to the fear rather than embrace everything else.

I began to make a list of the things that I could do if I chose to. The places that I could visit, the things that I could see, but most importantly, just that true feeling a gratitude that I had for the opportunities that lay ahead of me as well as those things that I was grateful for that I had learnt so far.

I was about to step into something that was totally different to everything my life had been based upon – I would say goodbye to my mom and my sister who had been a huge part of my life, as well as a huge support for me personally. For the first time in my life, I would now have to live and apply every single thing I had been working on, and it was a very big decision to make.

But I began to get excited. Deep down inside, I was like a little kid. I was making lists of things to do. I was imagining what it would be like to stand underneath the London Eye at night. I was preparing myself to navigate the underground system and wondering what it would be like to see snow. And every change I had, I was giving thanks for the opportunity I had which helped me overcome those moments of doubt when I wondered where I was going to live or how I was going to find a job.

I remember the day I left to start the next chapter of my life. The flight was delayed by a couple of hours and we all sat quietly at the airport. I did not know what was going to happen, as a friend of mine who lived outside London had stopped contacting me a few weeks earlier but I had been too afraid to tell my family just in case things change – they had, after all, seen me go through some of the worst times of my life and the fact that someone I knew was there to help me gave them a sense of relief. As you can imagine, I was pretty terrified, but my new way of thinking got me to focus on the excitement of what was to come and this gave me the courage to physically take the step into the unknown.

I landed at the airport after midnight and not knowing how the transport system worked, decided that it would be best to sleep on a bench rather than make my way into London. It also gave me some time to find a place to sleep for the next few days – after all, I had minimal money and just a bag to my name, and using the internet was something pretty new and unique to me.

I am not going to lie to you and say that it was easy, but I guess being like a kid in a candy shop has its amazing way of getting you through radical change. That excitement kept me going when it felt like all I could do was give up. When I slept at train stations for a few nights as I had run out of money was pretty intense, yet a deep sense of gratitude brought on that optimism to get up and keep going. I never stopped believing that one day I would be able to do what I dreamt of doing and my gratitude account kept me topped up and moving forward.

Over the next few days, which turned to weeks and then months, and now into years, every single challenge I took on was a "game" for me. Seeing the ondon Eye at night for the first time was truly eye-opening for me and visiting Hamley's reminded me to keep the excitement going.

And there were times when I forgot to have fun and gave in to the fear – many times actually.

After all, to me, it is all about learning and reminding myself that I am not the only one that has done this and there will be many more people who do take on challenges to change their lives.

That same excitement has opened my eyes again when I felt I was too scared to carry on, but more importantly, it makes things so much easier to deal with and I constantly need to remind myself of this fact.

5.3.9 T – TIME TO CELEBRATE

Celebrating triggers all those feel-good endorphins in your nervous system and gets you going, so if we take time out to celebrate each significant step no matter what the size, it will encourage the body and mind to stay focused and keep going during the tough times ahead, because after all, we want the tough times – these are what make us grow the most – and the celebrations along the way, to give us that extra storage and fuel for the tough times.

Are you ready to celebrate your success? What are you going to do to reward yourself when you get there? How are you going to celebrate and enjoy the small steps and learnings you receive along the way and enjoy the process of getting there? If we do not take time out to enjoy the journey, then achieving our promise is not going to be what we anticipate it to be – part of the whole process of celebrating is enjoying the ride and making the most of every event that comes our way.

At the end of every day, take time out to sit back and reflect on your process. Record your challenges and learnings, your achievements and successes, and before you go to sleep, be adventurous and write how excellent tomorrow is going to be. Get your mind in gear for the day ahead and let your subconscious celebrate how far you have come so far.

MY PROMISE :

HOW WILL I REWARD MYSELF WHEN I ACHIEVE THIS?

HOW AM I GOING TO REWARD AND CELEBRATE THE ACTION STEPS THAT I TAKE ALONE THE WAY?

HOW AM I GOING TO CELEBRATE MY LEARNINGS AND TEMPORARY SETBACKS?

CASE STUDY

JEROEN

Yeah I remember those days, the days of ongoing partying and ongoing recovery. First only on Saturdays, we would get together to organise where and who we would get the merchandise from. Sometimes a really frustrating event, if it all took too long and we couldn't connect with the people that we needed to. After getting what we wanted, we joined the rest of the group of friends and made our way to Club X, a club just over the Belgium border, away from the civilized world, where no people lived. People from different parts of Holland and Belgium drove more than 100 miles to get there sometimes.

In the Club they played Hardcore and Mellow House-music, which we were fans of at the time. The combination of the up-tempo music and drugs was quite an amazing experience. We danced and danced and danced and danced.

Then we would also go outside and sit in the car with some music on. Sometimes we even didn't get to the front door of the club, as we had too much fun and amusement going on in the car. And of course, for people that ever did E, you know that when you get in a comfortable position or place, you don't want to move.

Our group of friends became really close and we had a lot of fun. The Saturdays now became Fridays and Saturdays. Still - lots of fun, although the recovery phase took a bit longer. We also started to take more drugs, to get the same results and have the same experiences. We began going to different places, meeting new people and trying new things. One night we went to a place in Rotterdam called Parkzicht. Here it was pure hardcore and what I saw there scared me a bit.

It was already getting light outside and there were people everywhere, but especially in their cars. People that were on the same journey we were, only they had already been travelling for longer. They were ghostly white, dark marks under their eyes and skinny like beanpoles. They looked like zombies! I had the feeling that I was walking in a living graveyard.

It made me realise that we were heading in the wrong direction. But as you might know, knowing that you are doing something that isn't good for you is not always the trigger to make changes in that exact moment. Most of the time we go a bit further or deeper, before we make that change that is desperately needed.

So Fridays and Saturdays. They now became Wednesday, Friday and Saturday and we didn't sleep a lot, we took even more drugs to have any effect and the as for the other days, well, we just felt like crap. And so we would find other drugs to get through the down phases. The group also began to fall apart; people were lying to each other and everyone got paranoid, including me.

This is where everyone was on their own again. We broke ourselves down completely. We used all our positive vibes and good feelings. There was hardly any self-esteem left. It sounds very dramatic, but I can honestly say, that I am truly grateful that I had this experience. It gave me the chance to build up from scratch and it also gives me an understanding of when my kids get introduced to any drugs. It will make it possible for me to pick up signals, so I can be aware of what is going on.

I now know that the most powerful thing in life to help someone that lost track is warmth and love. Without that, some people get lost forever and no one deserves that.

So I realise that that wasn't a long lasting way of celebrating and I am now teaching myself to celebrate every gain, small or big. It does take practice, I realise. But I can also see that the more you celebrate, the more there is to celebrate in life.

GARETH

There was a time in my life when all I used to do was to focus on the things that did not go right. To say that I used to come down hard on myself is a bit of an understatement because no matter what I personally achieved, it was never ever good enough. I used to say to myself that it was because I really wanted to be the best at whatever it was that I chose to do, however, I guess you could say that it actually never really was that. Celebration was, and sometimes still is, something that I struggled with a great deal, especially when it comes to "mistakes."

Maybe it goes back to some far gone time in my life, who knows. What I do now is that it comes from me and nobody else. Celebration was not a word that existed in my dictionary of life until recently, and therefore I guess this is why this is the most challenging thing to write about.

In the past, celebration was an excuse to go out and get wasted, to go out and completely forget about every single thing that happened because after all, you deserved it right? Doing drugs was something that started from a very young age, and as I got older, was something that I did because it gave me the confidence to not give a shit about anything. I was not afraid to take anything or try the new stuff that came in, and besides that, I worked hard and I deserved it.

But I never could quite understand why I was always still going when everyone had passed out or gone home. And I also could not understand how, for them, it just was not normal to do this every now and then. I mean, why would you not celebrate the shit day that you just had by totally forgetting about it?

And despite all the amazing things that I had in my life, I let it consume me and take over so much of my life. Until it nearly killed me and I realised that something had to change because I couldn't even die properly. And so I stopped celebrating because deep down inside, I did not believe that I should. It may sound severe to take this approach, but I am sure it makes a bit of sense to some people.

Recently, I had the opportunity to go to Portugal to do my final training with a company I had been studying with for some time. For me, this was a pretty amazing achievement for many reasons. And I suppose that is was also the first time that I fully applied this final step to one of my dreams. I started my journey with this company about 2 years ago, and throughout every event I have attended, I have made, and taken, massive strides in terms of how I live my life.

It was with these people that I began to realise and accept the gift that I had been given, and where I finally made the decision to promise myself never to settle for less than I deserved.

You see, going to Portugal was something that I thought was for "other people" and something that I did not deserve. And this would be the first time, aside from moving to London some years ago, that I would ever be going to a foreign country. This in itself was a dream come true, but more importantly, it was the first time I allowed myself to celebrate every success I had made along the way, but more importantly than that, it was the first time I truly celebrated every so-called mistake and "wrong" choice and decision I had made too. To be able to allow myself to do this was a special thing.

As the training progressed, something deep down inside of me changed forever. And as each breakthrough came, in my own way, I silently celebrated. It was on the beach one night, when I was just sitting and giving thanks, waiting to catch up with Jeroen that I celebrated. As I think about it, can still feel the sand under my feet, the moon in the sky and I can hear the waves caressing the beach in that constant, relaxing way that they do.

But for me, it was during that week in Portugal that I realised that this could possibly be one of the most important steps in what this book is about. In the last 5 years, I have pushed myself to places I never believed I would be able to go. I have stretched myself far beyond what once seemed impossible, just so that I could put these steps to the test. And with each promise that I set myself, I found that by following them, things changed and things happened. And not just little things. Radical things.

To some, it may sound over the top and to others, it will make perfect sense.

I learnt that in order to achieve my big dreams and promises to myself, I have to make every day of my life a celebration of the fact that I have the chance to dream.

When I make celebration something that only happens on special occasions, something is different – and this is solely my opinion here and what I have found gives me the greatest results.

I learnt that when I celebrate everything, more and more happens for me in my own life and that is how I choose to do it now.

6. Conclusion

So now what ? You have spent a lot of time and effort in going through this book, thinking and writing, listening and reading, then all of a sudden, just like that, it comes to an end.

Unfortunately it does though. The book that is!

But what happens next is probably the coolest thing ever. Just like we said at the start, most people spend more time on their Christmas shopping lists than they do on their own lives.

So what happens after they finish their shopping list? They go shopping. They go out there, knowing exactly what they are going to buy, they have what they need and they have an idea of where they need to go to get what they want. Because they are prepared, the shopping trip is a lot of fun as they also know why they are shopping. The look on the children's faces when the open the presents, the warm and loving hugs from their families as they get their gifts and the grateful smile on the face of their best friend when they open that box.

It makes it all worthwhile at the end of the day because they also know, that being the kind person they are, that they too will get the chance to open presents and gifts chosen just for them.

And just like them, you now get the chance to go shopping. You spent an amazing amount of time and effort to get to this stage of the book – more than (and now we are just going to make up some figures for you) 95% of the population in the world actually do. But you know what the sad thing is? Some people get this far and don't go shopping. Some people say "well, that was fun" and close the book.

Of the remaining 5% that did make their lists, a shockingly small percentage of them actually go shopping. Now we know that these may not be totally true statistics, but we think you get the picture here and know what we are talking about.

All that is left now for you to do is to go shopping – for the life of your dreams. You have, written down in this book, most of the things that you need to do this. You know what you need assistance with. You know what you want to do. You know what you are going to do when you face those challenges that are bound to come up because you have your gratitude list to keep you going. But more important than any of this, you know why you are going Christmas shopping for yourself.

The only thing left for you to do now is to take action. Massive action towards creating the ever-lasting radical changes you want. You now have the chance to take the next step on your journey of personal excellence through self discovery.

Also from MX Publishing

Seeing Spells Achieving
The UK's leading NLP book for
learning difficulties including
dyslexia

Stop Bedwetting in 7 Days
A simple step-by-step guide to help
children conquer bedwetting
problems in just a few days

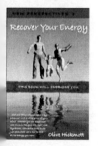

Recover Your Energy
NLP for Chronic Fatigue, ME and
tiredness

More NLP books at www.mxpublishing.co.uk

Also from MX Publishing

Play Magic Golf
How to use self-hypnosis,
meditation, Zen, universal laws,
quantum energy, and the latest
psychological and NLP techniques
to be a better golfer

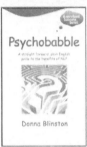

Psychobabble
A straight forward, plain English
guide to the benefits of NLP

You Too Can Do Health
Improve Your Health and
Wellbeing, Through the Inspiration
of One Person's Journey of Self-
development and Self-awareness
Using NLP, energy and the Secret
Law of Attraction

More NLP books at www.mxpublishing.co.uk

Also from MX Publishing

Process and Prosper
Inspiring and motivational book
from necrotising faciitis survivor
Wendy Harrington. Amazing book
for anyone facing critical trauma.

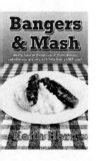

Bangers and Mash
Battling throat cancer with the help
of an NLP coach. Keith's story has
led to changes in procedure in
many cancer hospitals and is an
inspiration to cancer patients
everywhere.

Performance Strategies for Musicians
Tackle stage fright and
performance anxiety using NLP.

More NLP books at www.mxpublishing.co.uk

Lightning Source UK Ltd.
Milton Keynes UK
UKOW04f0245170114

224736UK00001B/5/P